SELF SABOTAGE NO MORE

Stop Repeating the Past and Start Creating Your Future

D0885000

JENNIE POTTER

Published by

SUCCESS IN

P A G E S
SHORT BOOKS. BIG IDEAS.

www.SuccessIn100Pages.com

ISBN 978-1-947814-47-9

Copyright © 2022 Jennie Potter

DEDICATION:

This book is dedicated to God who guides my writing and my family...

Dave, Hannah, Kai...

You are my EVERYTHING.

"Nothing and no one can complete you. You are already whole and complete exactly as you are right here and now."

- HALE DWOSKIN

Table of Contents

FOREWORD BY
RAY HIGDON

I first met Jennie a few years ago at a generic network marketing event for leaders. She later became one of our Inner Circle Coaches that work with our students who are serious about success. It wasn't until she reached out to me last year and asked if I could be her "guinea pig" as she tried a new method for helping people release trapped emotions that I knew how deep her work with people actually could go.

I agreed and was a little skeptical but still open-minded. I have done thousands of hours of personal growth with the best of the best and tried many different healing techniques to release the past and show up as my very best self.

I have openly shared that my childhood was extremely abusive. I was regularly abused as a kid and betrayed by my school counselor when I trusted them for help. I have worked hard at letting it all go so that I can have an extraordinary life and help others have the same.

After the first session, I felt different. Lighter, more energetic, powerful, and peaceful at the same time. I messaged her the next day asking if we could do more. I became obsessed with releasing all of it. Many of the emotions like anxiety, distrust, depression, and fear were from my 6-year-old self and all that I'd been through. We identified that I had 1906 unprocessed emotions to release.

After we released those, we continued to work together discovering old sabotage beliefs that we could release as well. We also began working on resetting setpoints that I had in areas such as weight, finances, belief in my ability to "have it all" and more.

Jennie is gifted in "seeing" other people's energy, their emotions, sabotage beliefs, and setpoints and it has been transformational working with her.

So, I was honored to support her to write a book and share the methods and techniques that have been instrumental in helping me break through my past once and for all.

Her goal with this book is to give everyone a recipe to help them release their own unprocessed emotions, sabotage beliefs, setpoints, and live their best lives.

This is a step-by-step guide for anyone who is fed up with sabotaging themselves, tired of setting a goal and not hitting it, procrastinating, and saying, "I'll start tomorrow."

I know for a fact that no matter how successful you might look on the outside—if you are still struggling inside, your work is not done. But there is help, and I believe this book is a must-have, must-read, and must-practice, on your journey to self-sabotage no more.

Ray Higdon

Best-selling author, coach, speaker, and philanthropist.

Introduction

When I was a little girl, I had a knack for understanding why people showed up the way they did. Even at a very young age, I looked at things differently. I could have been your friend for a year and not known what color eyes you had, but I could tell you about your emotions and your energy with my eyes closed. I was a walking "emotion sponge"—feeling everyone else's anger, sadness, and happiness—often taking it on as my own. I felt things more than I saw them.

I remember once walking right into a parked car and my mom asking me, *"What were you looking at?"* I didn't have an answer. I was in touch with what was happening and yet I was in my own world. I constantly daydreamed. I wanted to be a healer like Jesus, a writer, and an inspirational speaker. By the time I was twelve, my dream had turned into a more practical goal of becoming a counselor.

I was often anxious and was always drawn to the most uncomfortable person in the room and friends who were most wounded. I *felt* people instead of seeing them. I liked helping people and was a good listener and storyteller. I was an introverted extravert—I could put on social skills when needed but felt more comfortable with my nose in a book, alone and away from the noise of people and their emotions.

I preferred one-on-one friendships to groups and found parties stressful.

In high school, I learned to hide my heightened perception of energy and emotional skills and fit in using my more extroverted side. I learned to go with the flow and adapt to whatever emotion was present at the time. But, at a deep level, I felt out of place, like there had been some kind of mistake. I often talked to God, felt him in the wind, and somehow knew I had *"stuff"* to do. I spent a lot of time reading, writing, and sleeping. I always felt like I was missing something, wasn't seeing something, or that there was somewhere else I was supposed to be. I could never quite put my finger on it.

I felt lost.

In the tenth grade, my life took a bad turn. I was at a party. I had been drinking. A guy at the party lured me into the bathroom "to talk." I was still innocent and very trusting. I was unable to fend him off.

That night changed everything. I felt like everyone could see what had happened to me. I didn't want my parents to know. I didn't want anyone to know. I was ashamed.

On Monday, the boy bragged about what happened, acting as though it was consensual. I felt like no one would believe me that it wasn't. So, I didn't say anything. I shut down, emotionally. My innocence was gone.

I developed a deep distrust of people. Although it was not logical, I could not seem to forgive myself for what had happened. I had a conversation with God and knew I was to use what happened for good.

Still, I struggled with my definition of *self*. I felt unlovable, broken, and not worthy of being with a "good" person. I began to self-destruct. And so began my spiral of self-sabotage. Drinking. Drugs. Blacking out, waking up to empty containers of extra-strength Tylenol lying beside me over and over again.

"Self-sabotage is a sneaky and pervasive beast that shows up in many places."

I was a mess. I hung out with other people who were a mess. I stopped listening to any of my more conservative friends who gave me loving, positive advice. I was in a constant pattern of self-hate and abuse, and I could not stop. I couldn't get away from myself no matter how hard I tried.

There was no way out.

For many years the quote, *"Wherever you go, there you are,"* was my nemesis. The sad part is that I had incredible support. I *could* have talked to my parents. I could have asked for help. I had many friends and family members who saw a light in me—who loved me—and who knew that my behavior was incongruent with who I was.

I spent over a decade partying, experiencing blackouts, and making bad choices. I was the definition of self-sabotage.

As I share this, it feels like I am describing a different person. I see now with clarity who I truly am. Self-sabotage is a sneaky and pervasive beast, that shows up in so many places—from who we choose to share our lives with, to where we live, the jobs we choose, how much money we have in the bank, and our health.

It shows up in who we call friends and our daily habits. It shows up everywhere. It is not us. But it becomes us. That familiar comfort of being uncomfortable.

I have always maintained that being *in* the comfort zone was, in many ways, more uncomfortable than being outside of it.

So, why did I stay there?

As I searched for a way to climb out of the pit I'd dug for myself, connect with my purpose, and heal, I picked up a lot of tools along the way. Some were super effective, some not so much. I dove into everything. It was the only answer to finding myself again.

I attended university and got a bachelor's degree in psychology. I went to counseling college and earned a diploma. I became a certified coach with John Maxwell's speaking, leadership, and coaching program. I was obsessed with my self-sabotage tendencies and was intrigued to see them in my clients, my friends, and my colleagues.

I studied the physical body: massage, energy meridians, hands-on healing, crystals, human frequency, and meditation.

I read, listened, practiced, and prayed.

Eventually, I healed enough that I was able to start a business. I fell in love with the love of my life and am blessed with a healthy relationship. I left binge drinking and smoking behind me and started dreaming bigger. I began writing again. I learned how to speak on stage, stepped out of my comfort zone, and released the anxiety that had plagued me for most of my adult life. I was not fully healed, but I was getting there.

I went from broken, destructive, self-hating, self-sabotaging, depressed, lost, and practically penniless to being whole, abundant, confident, self-loving, purposeful and full of joy.

In the last few years, all the pieces have come together. I have discovered some powerful techniques to help people release their self-sabotage and step into who they truly are. I found a simple way to heal after thousands of hours of self-exploration and working with clients. It's a method that can help people simply and powerfully release their limiting beliefs around who they are, hit the reset button, and achieve new heights.

I am seeing clients transform and release more quickly than ever before. Through energetic and emotional release work (in as few as three to six sessions), I have clients who are transforming their self-worth, habits, and relationships. Their finances are increasing for the better, invisible blocks are crumbling, and they are creating their best lives.

The coming sections will give you a map and assistance in understanding, identifying, and then finally releasing the self-sabotage within you.

Whether you are reading this book because you are a little frustrated with not moving forward in a few areas of your life— or you want to stop sabotaging your personal or career success—or you feel broken, lost, alone, and like your soul is crying out for total transformation like I was, this book is for you.

-Jennie

P.S. You may have noticed that this book—like most books these days—contains one of those fine print disclaimers on the first few pages. But, in case you missed it, I want to make sure you know that I am not trying to diagnose or cure any kind of emotional, physical, or psychological illness. If you feel like you are a danger to yourself or others, please call 911 or the national suicide hotline.

I also want to acknowledge that we'll be talking about things like energy, vibration, feelings, and emotions, some of which may feel like "woo-woo" nonsense to you. I understand. I hear that a lot, especially from new clients. I ask only that you give the ideas in this book a chance. After all, you were open-minded enough to pick it up and start reading, right?

Don't stop reading and self-sabotage now—keep going. You got this.

Autopilot

When I was about 12 years old, my father took me on a two-night overnight stay in Mexico. He was a commercial pilot for one of the big airlines and treated me to the trip. The airplane we were on was a typical commercial jet. To make things even more exciting, I got to sit in the cockpit. (Note: This was before September 11th when this kind of thing was still allowed.)

It was an uneventful flight and so much fun just sitting in the jump seat staring at the big blue sky and beautiful clouds. It came time for us to begin our approach. Suddenly, an alarm went off, along with a computerized female voice I will never forget:

"Pull up, pull up. Terrain ahead, terrain ahead."

My dad spoke to me calmly but firmly: "JJ, do NOT speak."

I sat there, quiet as a mouse. I was at that age where I believed in my dad so completely, that I wasn't really scared. He was larger than life and could fix anything. But still, the alarm would not turn off.

"PULL UP, PULL UP.
TERRAIN AHEAD, TERRAIN AHEAD."

As I peered out the window of the cockpit at miles of empty sky before us, it was clear there was nothing ahead—but the plane was on autopilot—it was a glitch, a malfunction—and they could not shut off the alarm.

Suddenly, my dad announced: *"We are going manual!"*

With that, he shut down the computer and he and his co-pilot flew the plane *"old school,"* which meant they had complete control of the aircraft without the computer. My dad had thousands of hours of experience on every kind of airplane you can think of. He did what we are going to talk about in the coming sections. He had to turn everything off and find another way.

The truth is that many of us have been flying on *autopilot* for a very long time.

We're in the same patterns, same setpoints, same thoughts, same flight path, same destination, same unprocessed emotions... in a way, it's the same day, over and over. When we try and do something out of the routine our alarm goes off. It's a malfunction. It's a glitch. A false alarm.

But it goes off nevertheless, and we adhere. The usual program requires much less energy than the "detour" we want to take.

Frankly, the original destination was probably picked a long, long time ago by your 7-to-12-year-old-self, and you have been headed there ever since. This includes:

- I'm not worthy of success
- I'm not smart enough
- I'll never be happy
- I'll never fit in
- I'm not wanted
- I'm not special

- I'd better dim my light—when I shine, I hurt others
- Wanting money is bad
- I'll never be forgiven
- There's not enough time
- I'll never be organized
- I'm always late
- I'm destined for failure

And on and on.

As you dive into this book, you may notice that you have to reset the autopilot to a destination more desirable—one that your adult self has decided on. You may find you have to identify and release some of the unprocessed emotions you never dealt with. You are going to have to delete those sabotaging beliefs that are constantly "auto-correcting" your direction. We will have a look at your setpoints, too. Are you stuck at a certain financial setpoint? Relationship setpoint? How's your "having it all" set point?

"You have to reset the autopilot to a destination more desirable."

In the following sections, we will identify the hidden glitches, including unprocessed emotions, sabotage beliefs, and sabotage setpoints that might be holding you back and causing difficulties. We are going to shut it all down and manually bank right, moving with ease towards a new destination, a destination with intention, a destination of your choosing, a destination of your dreams.

The Decision to Change

Ever make a decision that was going to change your life? You are tired of the highway you have been driving on, tired of the same old day-in and day-out; it's time for a change, and tomorrow morning (no matter what), you are going to start!

- Get up early.
- Exercise before work.
- Eat differently.
- Make those sales calls.
- Send those messages.
- Get organized.
- Meditate.
- Start writing that book.

It feels great, doesn't it? You've made a decision!

"Tomorrow I am going to get off this highway and take an exit to Destination Healthy; Destination Wealthy; Destination Peaceful; Destination Eat Well, Get Up Early, Write Out Goals, Make a Dream Board," etc.

But tomorrow comes, and you don't do "the thing."

Instead, you hit the snooze button and sabotage the well-intentioned life change. Annoyed, puzzled, and frustrated, you decide, *"Next week I'll do it."* Then, *"I'll start in September."* Then, as September approaches, you find yourself saying, *"I think January first would be easier."*

In the end, you just never take that exit. Never hit that reset button. Never make that change.

You are not alone.

Millions of people have massive dreams and are longing for change. Millions of people have *tiny* dreams and are longing for change. And for some, tomorrow truly never comes.

What's the Secret Sauce?

What's the thing that's in the way, stopping you from shining your brightest? Getting in the way of you unwrapping your God-given, *born-only-to-you* gifts? What's keeping you in this monotony of mediocracy when you know you have so much more to give? So much more life to live. You so badly want to take that exit and get off this highway but you continue to self-sabotage.

Maybe you have done pretty well for yourself, having gone *all in* on personal growth. Perhaps you have even identified (to some extent) a lack of worthiness, fear of success, or a struggle with addiction. You *know* what's holding you back but still cannot seem to break through to that next level. Whether in business, sales, influence, relationships, health, or connection with the divine, you just aren't taking that exit.

Here's the good news and the bad news: *The struggle is real.* There *are* reasons for your inability to take those steps to make those changes. And let's be clear, this has very little to do with your level of desire and a lot to do with the *hidden sabotage factors* between you and what you want.

As a coach, I have worked with people who have had the same goal for years but it always seems out of their grasp. For example, they have wanted to lose 15 pounds for the last 30 years. They have wanted it, obsessed about it, and not achieved it for any sustained length of time over three decades. There is something (or perhaps more than one thing) that they just can't seem to make themselves do to take that exit off the known highway and familiar destination, to a new city, new place, new outcome.

Does this sound familiar to you?

No matter how hard you try, no matter how much you want it, you just keep sabotaging and veering back onto the same old path you have been on forever. The autopilot continues to correct to the original set destination. An original destination *by the way,* that you set years ago without understanding you were doing so.

When I found the "secret sauce" to help clients remove the shackles of inertia, procrastination, and self-sabotage, I was beyond excited. I used all of my training as a counselor, and coach, years of energy work, and special abilities to "see" and feel emotions to help people clear.

As we saw transformational success take place, I began to work on the "keys" of self-sabotage. These were the things I was explaining to clients in every session as well as in homework for when we finished our work together—tools that they could take to their families, coworkers, friends, and teams. That's what this book is all about.

Be warned. This will touch every aspect of your life should you apply it—your health, your finances, your happiness, and your relationships. So, buckle up because you are about to shut down the autopilot and go manual, flying to the destination of your choice.

What Is 'Autopilot'... and Is Yours On?

Autopilot isn't just for airplanes these days. Autopilot is used on trains, subways, cruise ships, sailboats, and computers— heck, even your phone is automated and *smart.* Your camera automatically adjusts its lens, and your bank app recognizes your face and remembers your preferences.

Autopilot is everywhere, even in *you...*

Your computer is, in some ways, set up like you are: *"The best guess from what we did last that stuck"* kind of way.

My computer still logs in to my daughter's Gmail account first because it's so "smart" that it remembers the one time she used it and sets it as a "favorite." Much to my frustration, when the kids borrow my car and set their phones to Bluetooth, it's so smart it remembers them and not me when I hop in, forcing me to listen to my tunes from my phone speaker until I can remember how to reconnect my own Bluetooth. In charge but not in charge.

You think you are driving but you are not exactly in control.

- Your *conscious* is the pilot, driver, and user.

- The *subconscious* is the "smart" automation, autopilot, and auto control.

What does this mean when we are making a change or creating a new habit?

On the most basic level, you need to be *aware* of the automation taking place. You also will want to be aware that you are not your automation. You are not your automatic thoughts (or any of your thoughts for that matter). Thoughts are just part of the program.

You are not your actions. Action or inaction happens because of your automated program and your "sabotage glitches" whether you intentionally programmed those glitches or not. The glitches happen because the conscious wants something different than the subconscious. The conscious mind is like a conductor (who thinks they're in control) that the orchestra (subconscious) is ignoring. Meanwhile, the orchestra "knows best" and is playing a completely different song.

The Subconscious Usually Rules

The big question we need to ask is, *why* does the subconscious usually win? It comes down to the nature of each. *Think iceberg.* Conscious is at the top, above water, and *sub*conscious is exactly what the word implies: down below, hidden.

The **CONSCIOUS** part of our brain is...

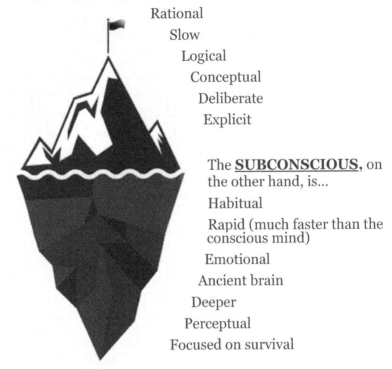

Rational

Slow

Logical

Conceptual

Deliberate

Explicit

The **SUBCONSCIOUS**, on the other hand, is...

Habitual

Rapid (much faster than the conscious mind)

Emotional

Ancient brain

Deeper

Perceptual

Focused on survival

Research suggests that the *conscious* is 5% or less of how we show up in the world. Meanwhile, 95% or more of how we show up is on the *subconscious* level, without our awareness.

What does this mean for us? Let's put it this way: You think you are driving the bus, but you are not.

Let's pretend you are driving a bus and you see an exit off in the distance that leads to "Success City" and decide to take that exit. The exit might represent a promotion in your company, weight loss, extra money in your savings account—whatever you're desiring in your life.

Everything is going along just fine, but—as you near the exit—your subconscious senses a change in you. It becomes alert.

You can think of change like this:

Change = Energy Expended

New roads take up more energy, and they represent potential danger and hurt from the times you tried different things in the past but failed. So, your subconscious—faster than a speeding bullet—deems the exit dangerous, grabs hold of the steering wheel, and...

You stay on the same old highway, left scratching your head, wondering why you procrastinated and got in your own way, got sick, held off doing something, or changed your mind, and didn't take the exit you knew you wanted to take.

The key to living the life you are dreaming of is to identify and become aware of these moments and reprogram the automation you no longer want automated.

Sabotage Anchors

What are sabotage anchors? Sabotage anchors represent forms of unprocessed emotions and sabotage beliefs.

Imagine you are on a beautiful sailboat that's state of the art and designed for comfort, speed, and adventure. Now imagine your sails are up and the wind is blowing, but you just won't budge or you are moving but painfully slowly.

Do you need to pull up an anchor?

Or perhaps many anchors?

Scott's Story

My client Scott was like this. Anyone who knew him could see that he had more than a few sabotage anchors holding him back.

Talented and funny, Scott appeared to others as successful and confident, yet deep down his inner saboteur was dropping anchor every time he tried to set sail. He had built his business up to where he had a large team and decent income but felt like he wasn't worthy of his success or of being a good leader. Every time he tried to change his circumstances, he was crippled with procrastination and self-sabotage. He struggled with setting boundaries with the people he loved, felt enormous guilt for not providing a steady paycheck, and struggled with what other people thought about him.

We spent a year attacking it from every angle. With tangible steps, creative brainstorms, and heartfelt conversations, we uncovered his purpose and set some boundaries, but the experience was painful and slow. He was having some success in business but not at the level he was hoping for. He could not seem to break free of the sabotage anchors holding him back.

Then one day, we decided to do some "release," a new form of coaching I was doing with clients to see if we could access his sabotage blueprint on a deeper level. It was completely different work than classic coaching and I was excited to see if this new method—something I had been working on with myself, my mentor, and a select few clients—would work for Scott.

Within two sessions of identifying and releasing unprocessed ("anchored") emotions, and a few underlying sabotage beliefs, things finally started to change.

We released anchored emotions around loss, vulnerability, self-abuse, feeling unappreciated and unsupported, defensiveness, confusion, terror, and indecisiveness. Some of these were stuck in processing from as early as age 1 through 15.

Scott sent me a message (I'll paraphrase) after the first session:

I woke up with more trolls on Instagram but oddly didn't care what they thought. I'm finally having conversations with peeps who are interested in my products, and it looks like I am going to be signing up a new team member soon. Things are shifting!

After the second session, Scott wrote: *I got this message right after our session from a person out of the blue who wants to work with me. I was also invited to travel with a friend and I was able to look*

at it neutrally without all my usual hesitation and emotional response and just decide it was a good move and say yes!

This was big. I was excited. We had moved forward exponentially faster than any other method we had tried. It was working! We had finally accessed and released the invisible saboteur energy and were pulling up anchors fast.

> *"You are divine.*
> *It's time to start*
> *being that.*
> *Quit pretending*
> *you're not."*
>
> **- PAMELA WILSON**

The quicker people can access the part of them that hits the snooze button when bigger dreams are on the horizon and delete them, the better.

Previously, whenever Scott had decided to pull up anchor and set sail, we stayed stuck or moved forward very slowly, but, after we removed a few anchored emotions in a couple of sessions, the anchors started coming up.

The good news is that *you* can pull up anchor, too.

Self-Sabotage Filters

Your filter, or your Reticular Activation System (RAS, for short) as the psychology folks call it, is another key component and a fairly big deal when it comes to your flight path. This part of the brain is "smart," like the apps on your phone. It tracks body movements, motor coordination, visual and auditory stimulus, breathing, and pain modulations.

It also plays a major role in consciousness like staying alert and falling asleep. And, most importantly for goal-setting purposes, it plays a central role in our conscious attention, what we let in and focus on while ignoring repetitive, meaningless stimuli around us. This last one is a crucial bit we need to explore and understand.

This is a very clever brain design. It's a real thing, and while all the science-oriented details on how it works are a bit too much info for the scope of this book, you need to understand how this little filter works.

Think about how a modern camera lens works. Because of the camera's brilliant design, it can automatically zoom in and zoom out, seeking out different focus points.

Now, think about your eyes. They also have lenses that work in the same way.

For a moment, look at something in the room and focus on it. Now, let in the rest of the room, and soften your gaze. What else are you letting in? What have you not noticed before? Find something blue. Did your gaze find something blue? Let in only blue? You just programmed your RAS to focus on certain things over other things.

The problem is our filter can sabotage us big time if we are unaware of how it works and don't use it properly, or rather, use it without intention.

"Change the way you look at the world, and the world you're looking at changes."

- MEL ROBBINS

Your RAS lets in what you have decided is a high priority while ignoring other things. Some of this is already set up for survival, like hearing your name in a crowd, or your baby crying at night, a loud noise that you are used to versus one which may signal danger.

If you took in every single detail of every single occurrence, place, thing, or noise happening, you would go into overload. So, in a miraculous design kind of way, your brain filters out what you don't need and keeps what you do. It lets in what *it* deems is important on a subconscious level—regardless of what you think (or even say out loud) on a conscious level.

This juicy little bit is what's key in learning how to manually turn off autopilot, then reprogram it. A bit like air traffic control for a pilot, air traffic control will only alert the pilot when there is something nearby. It won't alert the pilot of every take-off and landing happening, every plane in the air, and every circumstance, but rather only what will affect that specific flight path.

My husband and I bought a car a few years ago that got recalled. They made us an incredible offer—bring back the car, and we will pay you close to what you paid for it no matter how many miles are on it. We were pretty pumped. We are big "road trippers" and had put triple the normal amount of mileage on the car. Plus, I was excited because I wanted to get a small SUV that I was still comfortable driving size-wise but that I felt safer in. When we brought the car in to return it, we found a small SUV that was a couple of years old and nicer than anything I had ever driven before. It was a cute shape that looked different to me than other SUVs and to my delight, when we test-drove it, it felt like a car but had the height I had wanted. As a bonus, I had never seen this SUV before!

Although I didn't normally care about stuff like that, a part of me relished the idea of me driving something beautiful and unique. As we headed home, I saw another SUV like the one we just bought and then another. Over the next few weeks, I noticed them all over the place. Did I mention I had never seen one before? This is how your filter works. It lets in what's important to you. It lets in what you focus on. I had never let that SUV in before because I wasn't focused on buying one.

Whether or not you do so with intention, you set your filter. Your RAS then searches for proof to make that setting right.

In her book, "The High Five Habit," inspirational speaker and best-selling author Mel Robbins discusses the RAS phenomenon and suggests a simple exercise to highlight how it works by challenging readers to look for hearts in everyday life—in things like stones, leaves, and cappuccinos—and notice what happens. (Spoiler alert: you will see hearts everywhere!)

Training Your Brain

Personally, I love noticing number sequences and have trained my brain to find them. I see 888, 777, 222, 333, 444, and 1111 all the time. License plates, the clock setting, the odometer, phone numbers—everywhere.

A situation that has great meaning to me is when I see 444 because it immediately makes me think of my father. I literally look up and say, "Hey, Dad," and smile. For me, 444s represent protection, angels, and my dad.

> *"You cannot create a new reality while looking at your current reality."*
> - JERRY & ESTHER HICKS

For my dad, fours were a different story. *He* thought they were *bad* luck. This started because he had heard they were the symbol of death in another language.

One of my dad's flights had ended with the plane he was flying hydroplaning upon landing. When the plane finally came to a stop, past the end of the runway, the dashboard had a significant number of fours on it. No one had been hurt, and although it was very stressful at the time (in those days, pilots were suspended without pay, pending results of a full-scale analysis of what had happened, and a determination regarding who was at fault), the accident ended up creating a domino effect that led to the fixing of a significant design flaw of the plane he had been flying. It also cleared the names of a few pilots who had wrongfully been found at fault in previous occurrences.

When the investigation ended, I told my Dad that fours represented angels surrounding him and keeping him safe. For him, however, fours would forever equal bad news.

How to Start

Try setting your own RAS filter for something simple—like hearts or particular numbers or yellow cars, whatever—and start noticing what happens.

For me, the numbers have come to mean something. I have these little moments when I see three eights, and it means abundance. Seeing sevens means blessings, and twos mean balance. I feel in these moments that I am in alignment, that God has my back.

So, if you are someone who already notices every time the clock says 11:11, then give it some meaning like abundance is coming your way or you are loved. Power-pack your filter with the good stuff.

Changing Your Filters

This exercise will not only help you understand how quickly you can change your filter but also show you how much opportunity and abundance is out there if you look at things from a slightly different perspective.

Next, you can try setting the filter to:

- Money comes to me in many different ways.
- Healing is easy.
- Everything goes my way.
- I'm always upgraded.
- I am favored.

Your subconscious will always look for proof that you are right, and your filter will let in that proof to back up *your truth*. Alternatively, you may have some *sabotage filter* settings in place. For example:

- You are always disrespected. The *filter is set and looking for proof of disrespect.* The sabotage filter will eliminate and ignore evidence of respect.

- Money makes people evil. *Sabotage filter will bring to your attention rich, mean people* and will filter out anyone who has money and does charitable things (much like my "unique" SUV, you just won't "see" them.)

- You are not worthy of success. *The filter will help you notice and fixate on where you have failed*, you will not note where you are successful.

Do any of these sound like you?

Air traffic control (your RAS) will always alert you to information that proves and highlights *your* beliefs. For example, here is a story of how I unwittingly set up my RAS to *filter* luck into my life.

When I was in high school, I got it into my head that I was lucky. My friends used to say, "Jennie, you are so lucky," so often that I began to repeat it over and over. I described myself to myself that way, and I experienced luck all the time. I locked into the belief that it was a fact, that I *was* lucky. I still have that belief to this day, and you know what? I am.

> *"We're not in a world of information overload, we're in a world of filter failure."*
>
> **- MICHAEL LAZEROW**

Or am I?

Filter set for: *"Look for evidence of I am lucky."*

When I was 29, I went to a restaurant to meet with a couple of friends. I put on my stilettos, took a cab, and met them as they were leaving. As the three of us walked arm-in-arm (they were a little tipsy), we laughed as they leaned on me in the middle. When we reached the crosswalk, a police officer was talking to someone he had just pulled over. The police car blocked the view of the oncoming traffic, so I peeked out to see if anything was coming, with my friends hanging a few inches back. As I stepped out, a drunk driver sped out of nowhere, ran over my foot, and instantly knocked me to the ground. I literally did not know what had hit me. One moment, walking and laughing, the next moment lying on the road. The police chased the driver and called an ambulance. It all happened so fast.

Most people would think of being hit by a drunk driver as pretty unlucky. Not me. All I could think of was how lucky I was. Lucky to have my friends with me for support. Lucky to have the police right there. Lucky to be alive.

I'm not saying I enjoyed being run over, and the following days were hard. I was a massage practitioner at the time and could not put weight on my foot, so I could not work. With no savings and no income, things were financially rough. An X-ray failed to show the break in my foot and so the physical therapist had me jumping up and down and stretching. As a result, I did not heal and was in continuous pain.

But I'm Lucky

Eventually, the doctor ordered a different kind of X-ray. They found the broken bone and ordered surgery. I received a hefty payout from my insurance company from the driver who hit me. And, once the surgery was done, my healing took only a few months, and I was back to work.

The whole time I felt lucky; lucky the doctor ordered the second scan; lucky I had a good surgeon; lucky I didn't die; lucky I got a claim; lucky I managed to pay my bills and keep my apartment.

Lucky. Lucky. Lucky.

I'd set my filter to: *"Look for evidence that I am lucky!"* And I can't help but wonder what my experience would have been like had my filter not been set to *look for evidence of luck.*

Imagine, if back in high school, I had my filter set to look for evidence of being *unlucky.* "Air traffic control: Please only alert me of unlucky."

Suddenly, my whole story—my whole *life* story—would change in an instant. How could I be so unlucky to be hit by that car right then? Of all the moments for the cop car to block my view, the timing of the crossing, what are the chances? How could I be so unlucky that the doctor missed the broken bone in my X-ray, that I walked around on that broken bone for two extra months? That kind of unluckiness could *only happen to me!* I went months without work, without money, I was in constant pain, no one believed me, etc.

"Whether you think you're lucky or think you're unlucky, you're right."

Looking back at my "unique" SUV example, my hubby and I were lucky to have our car recalled. We got a buy-back at twice the amount we ever would have received had it not been recalled. But what if we had set ourselves up with a RAS setting of unlucky?

We would have complained to everyone, "How could we be so unlucky to buy the *one* car that gets recalled? We are the unluckiest people on the planet!"

So, What About You?

What does this mean for you? Well, have you ever heard the saying, *"Whether think you can or think you can't, you're right?"*

The same thing goes for luck. If you think you're lucky or think you're unlucky, you're right.

What things do you talk about? What do you believe? Do your filter settings and beliefs serve you? Or are your filters set to *sabotage*?

In the following pages, we will:

- Explore more ways to reprogram your filters and your autopilot
- Identify various "sabotage glitches"
- Learn ways to reprogram your destinations
- Discover how to step back into the manual driver's seat

We *need* the filter and the autopilot to live our best lives. The key is being aware they exist and uncovering the sabotage settings that trigger the false alarms in the first place.

Energy & Vibration

We are all made of energy. We are all transmitting energy. We are made up of subatomic particles.

Your body, your thoughts, your emotions, your false beliefs about yourself and the world, your destination, your home, your surroundings, planes, trains, roads, trees, music, your friends, and your flight plan are very much made of the same stuff. Building blocks of atoms, each atom vibrating at its own frequency—some atoms a very high vibration, some very low—but all the same, *everything* made up of the same stuff. Stuff we can't see and stuff we can.

"If you want to find the secrets of the universe, think in terms of energy, frequency, and vibration."

- NIKOLA TESLA

The vibration part is important to note. Like attracts like, and so whatever level you are vibrating at, you are attracting.

To go back to the plane analogy, this will dictate a smooth flight or turbulence along the way, how the plane handles unexpected bad weather, and the ease or discomfort of landing once you get there. Said differently, you will either attract turbulence or attract a smooth flight, attract engine troubles, or have no mechanical difficulty depending on your vibration.

We Are All Attracting, All the Time

If you were a spaceship, your vibration is your tractor beam. What are you pulling toward you? Your tractor beam is always on—attracting experiences, opportunities, wealth, scarcity, drama, peace, favor, lessons, premium parking spaces, disease, pain, etc. You are attracting things to you all day long, whether you intend to or not. Whether you believe it or not—whatever you have going on in your life right now, your career or lack of one, your success or lack of it, your relationships, your home, your life, and how you feel when you wake up is in direct response to your filter, your autopilot settings, and your *vibration.*

There are ways to shift your vibration up and ways to bring it down. Many of you have thought habits that keep your vibration high or low. Equally powerful in this category is what you say throughout the day, what your core beliefs are, the music you listen to, and your good and bad habits.

- *Whatever you think about, you bring about.*
- *Whatever you speak about, you bring about.*
- *Whatever you have beliefs about, you bring about.*
- *Whatever you vibrate about, you bring about.*

In his book, "Raise Your Vibration," author Kyle Gray perfectly describes energy this way: "There is one thing that psychics and scientists can agree on: everything in the universe is made up of energy. That includes you. Right now, there is energy moving through every cell of your body, every atom of the air that you're breathing, and every part of the chair that you are sitting on. Energy is alive. It's here and it's now. It's what we're made of, and it connects us to everything that was, is, and ever will be. Energy is a subtle vibration, but it moves quickly. It's completely neutral, but it responds to our emotions and actions, and we respond in turn."

We are aware of vibration and talk about it every day. For example:

- What does it feel like to be in a crowd versus an empty church?

- How does it feel to enter a room where there is laughter or one where a big fight broke out?

- How does it feel when the energy is palpable because someone is in "confrontation mode" in a meeting, or when something just doesn't *feel* right?

- How does it feel when our energy is low? What does sadness feel like compared to anger? Healthy versus sick?

We are aware of energy and speak about energy every single day.

Recently, I was explaining to a client who has had a hard time believing that how she shows up attracts her experiences. Her language is often negative, and I tried to describe energy in a new way. I suggested she raise her vibration by listening to higher vibration music (a simple hack for the experienced or the novice.)

I warned her not to listen to something too much higher than her current vibe or she might get irritated. I said, "Don't start with the song, *"Don't worry, be happy,"* (a high vibration song) and she blurted out, "I hate that song! It's so irritating." Well, now she knows why. We laughed, but the point was made.

The music you listen to is a great clue to the vibration you are currently in. If you are wanting to up your vibration so you attract something different, try on a different vibe. In later sections, I've included different ways to raise your vibration. You can also go to my website for my top suggestions of songs to listen to shift your vibe.

It's important to note that when you don't feel like doing vibration-raising exercises, it is the very time you need to do them. Raise your vibration, feel different, attract something different, and change your circumstances.

To eliminate self-sabotage, understand that your emotions, sabotage beliefs, and sabotage setpoints (we'll get to these later) all have a vibration of their own. So, if you don't like the way things are or you want more from life, pay attention to your vibrations. They are attracting, beaming up, and calling in your current circumstances, and it is completely in your control to change.

Sabotage Beliefs

Once you understand we are made up of energy and vibrations, and that we are running on autopilot and there is a filter, the next key is understanding the sabotage beliefs.

There are "glitches" that keep us off track or on the old track that we didn't even intend to be on in the first place. These "glitches" are what sabotage our autopilot and filter settings in the first place.

Glitch: (Low Vibration) Sabotage Beliefs

Okay, so I know earlier I called the alarm system that goes off when you attempt to make a change a "glitch." But in some ways, that's not entirely accurate. In some ways, "the glitch" is a miraculous design. A design for survival. Think of your subconscious as being an adhesive (sticky) for bad experiences—sticking to negative memories and events to keep you alive, to keep you from doing what might harm you, kill you, or make you feel uncomfortable.

As psychologist Dr. Rick Hanson puts it, "The mind is like Velcro for negative experiences and Teflon for positive ones."

Here's a super-simple example of how this is helpful for survival and not so helpful for making life changes or setting goals:

You are eight years old. You eat a handful of berries you find along a random pathway. The berries turn out to be poisonous and you get violently ill. Moving forward, your subconscious (which is lightning fast) creates a new response to any unknown berries with nausea and some anxiety.

Result: *You never eat poisonous berries again, and you survive!* Awesome design, right?

Now let's keep to the berry example but throw a few other variables in the mix.

You were not supposed to go down that path, your mother had told you to stay on the sidewalk—but you disobeyed.

> *"The mind is like Velcro for negative experiences and Teflon for positive ones."*
>
> **- DR. RICK HANSON**

Your younger brother also ate the berries and was in the hospital for a couple of days while recovering, which terrified you. You had collected some of those berries in a container to bring back to the family with pure joy, knowing Mom would be so proud. Instead, you were reprimanded, the berries were thrown away, and you were told, *"You could have killed your brother! Why don't you listen? I told you to stick to the sidewalk."*

Your subconscious is busy making everything mean something.

Filter (remember the RAS) is being set up to look something like this: Collect evidence (let in through the filter) + the following beliefs:

- Berries are dangerous. *Check.*
- Exploring is dangerous. *Check.*

- The world is unsafe. *Check.*
- I'm a bad boy. *Check.*
- There is no point in trying. *Check.*
- I ruin everything. *Check.*

Your RAS/filter is set up to look for proof that the above statements are true. Any proof will do. The filter is also set to ignore any proof that *does not* support the false beliefs.

Meanwhile, the autopilot is being programmed to avoid adventure, to see new opportunities as scary, that trying something new is pointless and painful, etc. To put it another way, the alarm will go off *("Pull up, pull up. Terrain ahead, terrain ahead.")* any time opportunity, adventure, or something out of the ordinary arises.

And so it begins, or rather continues, from infancy into the present; the "who we are and how we show up" is being programmed. The majority of psychologists agree, that by the age of 12, most children have landed on their core limiting beliefs (or what we have been calling "sabotage beliefs").

So, what are some of the most popular sabotage beliefs?

- I'm helpless.
- I'm worthless.
- I'm unlovable.
- I'm not enough.
- I don't deserve it.
- Fear of failure.
- Trying isn't worth it.
- Fear of success.

- When things are going well something bad will happen.
- Everything is my fault.

Releasing a Sabotage Belief

Last year, I worked with a client, Carrie Marie, who is a podcaster and entrepreneur. She was extremely consistent when it came to working on her commission-based side business. Every day she shared her product, posted on social media, followed up with people who might be interested in learning more, and posted videos on TikTok to create curiosity. Oddly, however, Carrie Marie felt stuck. She had an extremely positive attitude and had added meditations and affirmations to her routine. On top of her side business, she is a wife, mom, and cat mom. She also has a full-time job in the web development arena. I had never had a client like her. She always did her homework, she was extremely consistent and productive, and yet, still no results.

After many sessions together of looking at what might be causing Carrie Marie's business to stay stuck, I asked her if she believed she was worthy of success. She answered, "yes" in her positive and cheerful way. Puzzled, I asked her if anything "big" had ever happened to her when she was a child, something that might be holding her back. She paused then she said, "Well, I don't think this could be it, but there was this one thing that happened when I was 12."

She went on to tell me her story:

CARRIE MARIE'S STORY

Carrie Marie had, what she thought was, a perfect life at age 11. A beautiful home in the country, friends, cats, sheep, bunnies, a school she loved, a church family, and a horse that doubled as her best friend. One day, out of the blue, she found out that her father was going to prison the week of her 12th birthday. They would have to move out of their home and leave almost everything behind. At that moment, everything changed.

Carrie Marie quickly had to adjust to a new life. She, her mom, and her sisters moved to a different town and went to a different school and church. She had to say goodbye to her horse, sheep, bunnies, some of her cats, her home, her father, her church, and the friends she knew, with very little notice, a lot of confusion, and some shame and heartache.

Carrie Marie felt she had to help her mom and sisters cope, so she put a smile on and acted like everything was okay. She never got the chance to grieve the shock and loss of it all. Additionally, deep down she created the core belief that success equaled pain. If she "had it all," the "all" could be taken away. Energetically, she was not in alignment with experiencing success. "Just enough" felt safer than "having it all."

"Beliefs are the lenses in which you interpret the world."

- JOHN ASSARAF

Once we identified this and processed the emotions around it, released the core limiting statement that *success equaled pain*, and walked through a visualization of making room for success, everything changed. Carrie Marie had a TikTok video go viral a couple of weeks into the sessions and had hundreds of people reach out and ask her for more information. She began bringing in new clients and business partners consistently every week about a month after the video was released. Because of that, she was asked to do TikTok trainings for her company and other groups and began to be invited to special events.

Carrie Marie released the limiting belief, processed her feelings, and transformed how she felt about her business. All this had the added benefit of relieving her ongoing back pain and discomfort, which she'd been experiencing for over a year. Negative and unprocessed emotions can cause real physical pain, often chronic.

When the "Glitch" Pops Up

The "glitch" pops up when we attempt to do something miraculous and game-changing, and it triggers one of our sabotage beliefs—those sticky limiting ("I'm not worthy, success hurts, there's no point in trying") false beliefs. We try to bank right or left, but that alarm goes off: "PULL UP. PULL UP. TERRAIN AHEAD. TERRAIN AHEAD."

We autocorrect ourselves with self-sabotage, procrastination, indefinite delays, and negative self-talk to get us back on course to *Destination Limited*.

Most of us are flying around, completely unaware of the autocorrecting we are doing. Most of us think we are in control and yet are baffled by the quiet self-saboteur within, keeping us small.

Think about it this way:

An alarm goes off to alert you that there is a problem. Let's look at your smoke detector. Your smoke detector is not smart. It goes off whether the toast is burnt or the house is burning down. It knows there is smoke. That's the extent of "smartness." How you respond is what could be different.

Every time the smoke detector goes off in your home, do you run screaming for the door, or do you check first? Essentially your subconscious sets off an alarm but if you/consciousness are aware it *might be a false alarm* or it is a false alarm, then you can reach up and hit the reset button instead of running away from burnt toast like it's a house on fire.

Sometimes it's just burnt toast!

Unprocessed Emotions

I t's time to discuss the most important part of the book, which is the topic of *unprocessed emotions*—and, more importantly, how to release them.

We hear about repressed anger all the time, see people holding back tears, and read stories about pent-up emotion and road rage. Entire industries are based on evoking emotions. Selling any product relies on emotions.

"Entire industries are based on evoking emotions. Selling any product relies on emotions"

We hear about people stuffing their emotions with food, escaping their emotions with video games, and avoiding their emotions with alcohol and other addictions. Workaholics stay busy so they don't have to face their feelings.

On a tangible level, we feel emotions, we know what someone is talking about when they bring up fear, anger, love, joy, or sadness but what are they? How do we know we are feeling them?

The simple answer?

Vibration.

A pulse.

Each emotion has a unique vibrational frequency. Low-frequency pulse equals sadness. High-frequency pulse equals joy.

You already know this. You know what anger *feels* like. You smile when you think of a funny moment and can feel that higher vibration bubble up and out. Have a sad thought, and you trigger a lower pulse.

A specific pulse creates a response.

You might feel it in your gut, your chest, or your head. Have you ever felt nervous and suddenly weak in the knees? Overwhelmed and feel lightheaded? Feel guilty and sick to your stomach?

This is frequency!

Frequency creates a chemical response in the body that releases *good-feeling* and *bad-feeling* chemicals, which in turn create what you understand as "the feeling." Whether that is an anxious one or a happy one, depends on the *pulse*.

Eileen Day McKusick, pioneering researcher, writer, and educator in the fields of therapeutic sound, the human biofield, and electric health, describes emotions as electromagnetic. McKusick uses tuning forks to detect trapped emotions in people's energy fields, current, past, or underlying.

In her book, "Electric Body, Electric Health," she discusses the research uncovered at the MIT computer science and artificial intelligence lab, where they created a device that uses radio waves to detect human emotion. The emotion recognition device known as EQ radio works much like her tuning forks—a lot like a dolphin or a bat uses echolocation navigation. EQ radio bounces wireless signals off a person and analyzes the signal that comes back. Radio waves are impacted by human vibrations and can detect changes in a person's emotional state.

What Is an Unprocessed Emotion?

When I first started doing release work with unprocessed emotions, many people responded with skepticism. I think this was because the thought of a ball of emotion physically *stuck* somewhere in the body causing physical and emotional damage was (and is) a little outside the box.

It's like one of those things hidden in plain sight. As we just discussed, we are all aware of our emotions and speak of them. We feel them as physical, describing them as a weight or a gut punch, butterflies in the stomach, or a confused feeling in the head when overwhelmed. We speak of a red flash or white heat when it comes to anger, but somehow, we have not given these very physical signs and symptoms tangible form.

Eckhart Tolle describes unprocessed emotions as built-up pain that is a negative energy field that occupies the body and mind—an invisible entity. It's what he calls the "emotional pain body," which may or may not be dormant causing some people to live their entire lives through the lens of the pain body. Other people may only

"Not only do you have these unprocessed emotions inside you, they vibrate and act like a tractor beam."

experience it situationally when specifically linked to emotional hurt.

In his book, "The Power of Now, he says, "Every emotional pain that you experience leaves behind a residue of pain that lives on in you. It merges with the pain from the past, which was already there, and becomes lodged in your mind and body."

If an emotion is stuck pulsing away inside of you, how do you get rid of it?

Often when I ask clients, "Where do you feel that fear?" or "Where are you feeling procrastination?" there is a slight pause. It's as if they have never considered this before but after a moment, they can give me a precise response.

Throat. Chest. Head. Knees. Pit of my stomach.

Most clients could assign their emotions with colors, and even describe the size if asked. Because emotions are physical in the same way music is physical—we hear it, feel it, sense it, and know it is real, even if we can't see it.

Are emotions real?

Yes.

Do they get stuck or interrupted in processing?

Yes.

Do they affect how you show up and interact with people and your relationships? Your goals, career, and procrastination tendencies? Your thoughts, autopilot, filter, air traffic control, triggers, and your perception of events—your everything?

Yes.

If you are one of the lucky ones, you were taught how to welcome feelings, not judge them and let them bubble up and out. But if you are like most of us, you were taught what society accepts and doesn't accept around emotion. You may have been raised by emotionally stunted parents or surrounded by unpredictable events. Or you didn't like the feeling of lower-energy emotions and stuffed them down (unwittingly hanging onto them).

Regardless, chances are you have at least a couple hundred emotions, if not more, all bottled up and stuck inside you. And not only do you have these unprocessed emotions inside you, but they also vibrate and act like a tractor beam, bringing more of the same.

The most beautiful and tragic description of unprocessed emotions I ever heard was that a trapped emotion was like a sad song stuck in your mind, playing over and over. So, when you think about two hundred or more songs playing at the same time—some loud, some softer—it's a miracle we get anything done! Soon, I'm going to show you how to discover how many of these unprocessed emotions (what I call your UPE score) you have and how to release them once and for all.

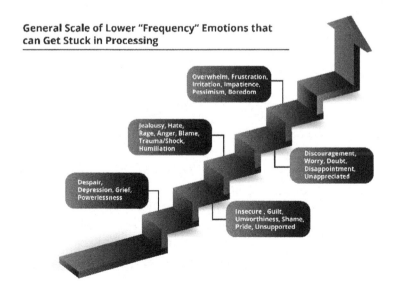

General Scale of Lower "Frequency" Emotions that can Get Stuck in Processing

Overwhelm, Frustration, Irritation, Impatience, Pessimism, Boredom

Jealousy, Hate, Rage, Anger, Blame, Trauma/Shock, Humiliation

Discouragement, Worry, Doubt, Disappointment, Unappreciated

Despair, Depression, Grief, Powerlessness

Insecure , Guilt, Unworthiness, Shame, Pride, Unsupported

How Emotions Get 'Stuck'

L et's go back to the example of the 8-year-old who wanders off the path and finds the poison berries.

You are 8 years old and eat a handful of berries you find along a random path. They are poisonous, and you get violently ill. Moving forward, your subconscious responds to any unknown berries with nausea and some anxiety. The result is you don't eat poisonous berries again, and you survive.

"Your subconscious is super busy trying to make sure everything means something."

You were not supposed to go down that path. Your mother had told you to stay on the sidewalk, but you disobeyed. Your younger brother ate the berries, too, and was in the hospital for a couple of days, recovering, which terrified you. You had collected some of those berries in a container to bring back to the family with pure joy, knowing Mom would be so proud... instead you are reprimanded, the berries are thrown away and you are told, *"You could have killed your brother! Why don't you listen? I told you to stick to the sidewalk."*

Now, as we already discussed, your subconscious is busy trying to make sure everything means something.

- Berries are dangerous. *Check.*
- Exploring is dangerous. *Check.*
- The world is unsafe. *Check.*
- I almost killed my brother, I'm a bad boy. *Check.*
- There is no point in trying new things. *Check.*
- I ruin everything. *Check.*

Add to this, the emotions you had around the event. You were scared... but because your mom reprimanded you, your **fear got stuck** in processing. You wanted to cry and be hugged but, instead, you were sent to your room to think about what you'd done.

- Fear (pulsing at a low vibration) = **STUCK.**
- Anger (with no way to express it) = **STUCK.**
- Confusion (about what was happening) = **STUCK.**
- Worry (you didn't mean to hurt anyone) = **STUCK.**
- Blame (you had no one to talk to) = **STUCK.**

And so it goes.

Stuck.

Stuck.

Stuck.

Releasing Unprocessed Emotions

How does all the stuck stuff that happened to you earlier in your life affect you today?

Have you ever noticed how different people react differently to the same situation?

Maybe something fires you up but no one else cares. Or your friend is super mad, and you don't get what the big deal is. Or maybe your parents or siblings trigger you when you spend the rest of your existence fairly trigger-free.

Let's look at the following example to highlight how our unprocessed emotions show up in day-to-day life—and how our false beliefs are lingering somewhere in there, too.

A boss addresses a five-member team. He says, "I've noticed the team is not commenting on social media posts. I would love some more participation from the team leading up to our big event!"

For the sake of the example, let's pretend each member of a five-person team has commented on one post per day for the last week. Here's how different team members react:

Team Member #1 feels immediate fear.

"Oh shit. He's mad at me for not commenting enough."

The alarm goes off. The fear that was trapped at 8 years old, when he was reprimanded by a friend's authoritative parent for accidentally breaking a lamp, gets lit up. The meeting feels terrifying. It's highly likely that some sabotage beliefs get triggered here, too. I'm an imposter. I'm not worthy to be on this team. He gives up a little bit and barely posts as he feels like he's already lost.

Team Member #2 feels humiliated.

"Yeah, he's right, I could be posting more, I better put that in my day timer so I don't forget."

Feeling like she failed, she is lit up for the rest of the day due to unprocessed emotions locked in at the age of 10 when a teacher pointed out she hadn't done her homework to the whole class.

Now, those sabotage beliefs are triggered: *"I'll never be organized, I am a failure, and everyone hates me."* She makes a serious effort to post more and feels a little sick about it each day leading up to the big event.

Team Member #3 instantly feels guilty.

"I'm on the case! I'm going to post more than anyone else!" Excited to be part of the team and promote the event. Guilt is lit up from the original moment at age 9 when Mom had put him in charge of helping around the house when Dad went away for work. But when he only did one load of laundry, he found her crying in a pile of clothes that she couldn't handle by herself. He also collects more evidence for the sabotage belief that says, *"I'm not reliable, I'm always letting people down,"* then promotes the event twice as hard.

Team Member #4 feels angry.

"I cannot believe he is talking to us like this. How dare he shame us!" Extreme irritation gets lit up from when she was 5 years old, cleaned her room but her brother's room was messy so they both didn't get to go to the beach. She has a sabotage belief that has her thinking, *"I'm unappreciated, there is no point in trying, and life isn't fair."* She decides to stop posting at all leading up to the event and instead starts making passive-aggressive comments in her social media feed shaming "toxic" bosses with high expectations.

Team Member #5 is unaffected.

This team member released his unprocessed emotions and limiting beliefs a couple of weeks ago. He thinks, *"Okay, the boss wants us to post more."* He makes a note, continues with the day, and posts more leading up to the event as instructed.

Releasing unprocessed emotions can help you excel in many areas of your life from how you wake up in the morning to how you treat others, whether or not you set a goal, how you interpret a text message, or respond to a friend not calling you. Unprocessed emotions can be the reason or source of physical pain: blocked sinuses, skin conditions, headaches, and chronic issues. They can keep you stuck in the same place and seemingly hide in plain sight quietly tripping you up and frustrating your attempts to live your best and happy life.

ANU'S STORY

I had one session with Anu. We released a few emotions that had been unprocessed and in her space for a long time. We checked for any blocked emotions around the topic of finances and the "loudest" emotions. This is typical for a session—we look for the loudest for the client's highest good, so that they may shine their brightest and unwrap all their God-given gifts. (Yes, I include God in these sessions as I believe prayer and intention make everything more powerful.)

Sometimes clients bring up topics such as lawsuits or finances, sometimes health or career, relationships, or buying a home. Nothing is off the table. We checked to see if something was blocking the flow of abundance into Anu's life. She had always had an ease with abundance and lately had felt stressed and blocked. As we released the unprocessed emotions, she immediately felt lighter. After our session, she felt as if a huge weight had been shifted. Within a week of our appointment, a check showed up in the mail out of the blue owed to her from five years earlier and positive opportunities were flowing her way. In her words, it was as if a locked door had suddenly opened, and abundance was flowing in.

My Experience with Migraines

I had struggled with migraines for over 10 years. I did everything I could to get rid of them. Sometimes a supplement would give me relief for a few months and then they would start again and throw me off my schedule for days at a time. I couldn't drive or work and felt like I was letting everyone down all the time. Plus, I'm not sure they truly understood.

Then I released my unprocessed emotions connected to the migraine using a process called unpacking which we'll discuss later. I released at least 10, which all felt like they were located in my right temple. Betrayal, rage, resentment, abandonment, fear, terror, insecurity, and more. I identified and released one after another. I have not had a full-blown migraine since that day. By my conservative estimation, I had already lost three to five days a month for 10 years give or take a month. Over 2,600 days of pain then—just like that—it was over.

Not only do unprocessed emotions cause problems with our filters and autopilot settings but also physical symptoms like I had. I've seen joint pain, sinus pressure, vertigo, shoulder pain, plantar fasciitis, skin conditions, and more, disappear with the identifying and releasing of stuck emotions.

(Note: Once again, I am not a medical doctor and not suggesting this will work for you, and I always recommend consulting a doctor. I'm simply sharing my experience.)

Emotions vs. Feeling 'Things'

Something I find very interesting is how we are taught to identify with emotions. For example, consider the difference between the statement *"I am angry"* versus *"I am experiencing the feeling of anger."* We speak as if we *are* the emotion:

- I *am* angry.
- I *am* depressed.
- I *am* anxious.

Expressing emotions this way makes no sense. For example, when you have a stomach ache, you don't say, *"I am stomach ache,"* do you? In other languages when you directly translate "I am sad" it sounds like, "I have sad," which makes more sense and does less damage. It puts the speaker in observation mode versus *becoming* the emotion.

The next time you feel anxious or some other emotion, instead of *becoming* it and *identifying* with it, just try being *aware* of it. Have curiosity about it. As much as you can, step back and separate yourself from the emotion. Become the "observer." Then ask yourself, *"What do I want to feel?"*

A powerful hack (this one always makes me laugh) is to say: "Body is feeling anger," (or whatever emotion you are experiencing at the moment.) This tends to not only add lightness to the situation but also buffers and gives space between the emotion and our awareness.

Instead of, "I am angry/pissed/irritated/depressed/sad," say *body* is angry; *body* is pissed; *body* is irritated; *body* is depressed; *body* is sad.

The first time I tried this it made me laugh. I had a long day—something like 16 back-to-back meetings and calls, with barely time to grab a glass of water. Normally my husband works away from the house and because I work from home, I usually handle the meals. I texted him and asked if he would order something for dinner because I was super hungry and tired. When I came out of my office into the kitchen, he was coming in from outside, and I watched him remember my request as he saw me and knew there was no meal on the way.

"As much as you can, step back and separate yourself from the emotion."

I felt irritation rise inside me and I turned to scavenge something for us out of the fridge. He saw my face and asked, "Are you super angry at me?" I paused, took a deep breath, and said, "Body is angry." We both started laughing. This simple change in approach made me realize I wasn't angry, just a bit *hangry*. I always laugh when I think of that moment.

But on a more serious note, what it did was separate me just for a moment from being *in* the anger and gave me the option to choose how I wanted to feel.

I had a client who often felt fear and then procrastinated whenever she looked at her list of people to reach out to. When we dove into what that felt like, we discovered a difficult memory connected to her father and a list of names of people who wouldn't help him during a hard time. Once we identified where the fear was coming from, it was easier to become aware of it and then observe it, understand it, and work with it.

I believe as a child, I saw and felt anger in others and knew I never wanted to treat people that way. Anger scared me. So every time something happened that could have sparked an angry response, I pushed it way down and said I was fine. It was fine. I wasn't mad. I never get mad. Ask me 20 years ago and I would have told you I could count on one hand how many times I had been angry. I would brag about a seven-year fuse. You could poke me for seven years and it would take me forever to get mad. But then out of nowhere, I would blow up—and *I hated it*. After an anger episode, I would feel shame, sadness, and failure.

I judged my own anger. I judged my inability to stay peaceful.

When I was first exploring the concept of releasing repressed emotions, it was because I was aware I had a lot of anger deep down. It was rare that I got angry, but when I did, it always felt disproportionate to the circumstance.

Through years of counseling training and exploration, I knew I had repressed anger but never really found a tool that helped me release it.

Pointing to the Past

Finally, I decided I was ready to solve this. I hired Tim Shurr, unconscious beliefs specialist, mind coach, and best-selling author, for some one-on-one hypnotherapy. I knew I had old stuff locked away and I wanted to be done with it. We discussed my deep-seated unpredictable anger. I could feel it deep in my belly and was ready to have it gone.

He asked me to point to the past. I was confused. He asked, "Is it up? Down? In front? To the left, right, or behind you?" He meant for me to literally physically gesture to where "the past" was for me. I said, "Behind me." He said, "Okay, take your hand from about the chin area in front of your face and make a sweeping motion up and over your head."

It was a simple exercise and it worked!

Feel the anger and put it in the past. I was to speak out loud three times whenever I sensed the anger feeling in the pit of my stomach—while making that hand gesture, "In the past, I felt angry but now I release it behind me." The work we did together helped me have a concrete *physical step* to take when I felt upset.

Instead of just searching for sabotage beliefs with clients, I began to search for unprocessed and repressed emotions as well. I created a process called the ALARM method. I do this with clients, walking them through the identification of unprocessed emotions and sabotage beliefs, then helping them release with awareness, and curiosity, and finally replacing those emotions with an affirmation.

Additionally, we began using a physical movement I call "unpacking" which in many instances was all that was needed to release the stuck energy. It worked particularly well with something "sticky" or tough to release.

Physical movement and paying attention to your body are important parts of this process. We'll talk more about how to get your body involved using a technique called, "muscle testing." But first, it's time to learn how you can use the ALARM method yourself. Once and for all, let's reboot the program, reset the autopilot with intention, and expose and delete those darn glitches that pop up every time you decide to make a change.

The A.L.A.R.M. Method

The first thing to be aware of when it comes to releasing repressed, unprocessed, pent-up emotions is that it doesn't have to be a long, drawn-out process. This can be as easy as letting air out of a blow-up mattress. Instant. This instantaneous release is natural and how it is meant to be.

Emotions are meant to alert us that something is up and then they are supposed to rise up and out. Where we get stuck is when we resist, tense up and accidentally hold on to that which doesn't feel good. We mess with the natural process by resisting or pushing down. This happens when we are not able to express our emotions and we learn what is acceptable and not acceptable.

Imagine a float tied to an anchor underwater. That's your trapped emotion. Time to cut the rope. Let it rise. Picture a balloon floating away when you release it. It is that easy. Once we have identified a trapped emotion, if we want to let it go once and for all, we need to welcome it, relax into it, "unpack it," and just like that, it will release. Contrary to popular belief, hitting pillows and yelling does not release emotions; it rather exacerbates them, keeps them stuck, strengthens them, and continues to light up the old original repressed ones.

The trick is to welcome rather than avoid, expand rather than contract, to open up and release instead of tightening the grip. Sounds easy in theory... but how?

I have created a five-step method for you to release unprocessed emotions. You can use this the moment you experience a strong emotion or to access past emotions that got stuck in processing. I call this "The ALARM method," and it is a simple process you can use effectively and efficiently to release the stuff that's holding you back.

"This can be as easy as letting air out of a blow-up mattress. Instant. This instantaneous release is natural and how it is meant to be."

It stands for...

A – AWARENESS

L – LOCATE THE FEELING

A – ASK YOURSELF THE QUESTION

R – RELEASE

M – MANTRA

A: AWARENESS of the feeling/thought/belief.

We start with awareness of feelings or thoughts. This part is key. Notice when you are feeling (irritated, sad, frustrated, or anxious) or when you are having negative thoughts.

It's important to note that working on the skill of awareness will help you in every area of your life. In truth, you *are* awareness. You are not your body. You are aware of your body. You are not your feelings, you are aware of your feelings, you are not your thoughts, you are aware of your thoughts. Being able to step back and be curious about your experience, versus becoming it, will help you shift into a gentler way of being. The practice of awareness and this concept itself is a whole other book, but for now, practice asking yourself throughout the day:

What am I aware of?

What is this awareness noticing?

Be curious about your thoughts, your feelings, and your beliefs. Ask the questions:

Am I that feeling? Or am I aware of that feeling?

Am I that thought? Or am I aware of that thought?

Increasing awareness will help you process and heal from the inside.

L: LOCATE the feeling.

Where are you feeling it in your body? (Stomach, chest, head, knees?) There is no right or wrong answer here, but we always feel our emotions in our body—that's how we know we are feeling them. Locating will help you release it and also increases awareness for the future.

Try this exercise sitting.

Begin by bringing your attention to your body.

You can close your eyes or keep them open, whichever is more comfortable.

You should notice your body, wherever you're seated, feeling the weight of your body on the chair, on the floor.

Take a few deep breaths (in through the nose out through the mouth.)

You should notice the sensations of your feet touching the floor—the weight, pressure, vibration, and heat.

Now, work your way from your feet, up your legs, to your hips, to your stomach, chest, arms, shoulders, neck, and head.

- Where are you feeling this emotion?
- When you become aware of the location, notice and think:
- Is it heavy? Light? Painful? Tight?

Be aware of your whole body as best you can. Take a breath. And then when you're ready, you can move to the next step.

A: ASK yourself.

Get curious. When have I felt this before?

If nothing comes to mind it's okay, just go to the next step. But if something pops up—even if it seems random, be curious about it—and acknowledge it.

Often our feelings come from old, stuck emotions tied directly to the original occurrence of that belief or emotion. If we can be aware of and release the original unprocessed emotion, we can sometimes in a moment release hundreds of negative thoughts connected to that old, unprocessed feeling.

The key here is curiosity. Wonderment. Too often we harshly judge our memories, feelings, and thoughts. What if you were just curious and asked yourself, "Hmmm...Where did that come from?"

R: RELEASE, allow the feeling to expand, then unpack.

We don't have trapped joy because we let it bubble up and out. But we unwittingly resist uncomfortable feelings and emotions and, as the saying goes, *whatever you resist, persists*. So, allow. Kind of like not tensing but relaxing into a headache.

I was in counseling school when one of the teachers suggested I welcome anger to release it. It felt impossible to welcome a feeling, I didn't like. To welcome a feeling I had spent years fearing. To welcome a feeling that to me, represented bullies and abusers. I tried. But it was all trying. It was over a decade later that I learned a tangible way to allow and release, both for myself and my clients.

How to Release and Unpack

(Note: You can do this standing or sitting.)

First, breathe in through the nose and out through the mouth. Do this at least 3 to 10 times.

Now open your arms wide and welcome the feeling, physically put your hands straight out in front of you and open them up like you are welcoming someone into your home.

Do this with the breath, do this with a smile, and *welcome the feeling*.

This movement automatically puts you in a welcome frame of mind. The physical movement will become connected to the release.

Now use a method I call "unpacking."

This is a sweeping movement almost as if you are wiping cobwebs off your body. Move your right hand down your left arm from shoulder to wrist with the intention to release the identified emotion. Then do the same with your left hand on your right side. Do this three times for each arm (you can alternate or do one side at a time).

I call this movement unpacking because you are clearing out space—literally unpacking energy that is blocking your natural flow.

Think of coming home from a trip. As you empty your carry-on you notice it smells weird; upon further inspection, you find an apple that you had packed a couple of weeks ago for a snack and forgot about. (How have you not noticed this?) It's stinking up the rest of the clothes and memorabilia. Do you shove it back in the bag and put it away for later or do you deal with it at that moment?

Exactly. Deal with it. Unpack it.

Notice what it feels like to unpack and allow it. This should feel like an expansion, not a contraction. A physical relaxing of the muscles in whichever location you have pinpointed the emotion/belief. The emotion/belief (and all the thoughts attached to it) releases like steam from a pot. (You can picture lifting the lid of the pot.)

It's that simple.

M: Mantra.

Pick something to replace the bad feeling/thought/belief.

When we release the unprocessed emotion here, we are releasing a lower vibration, making space for a new vibration of your choosing. It's a bit like cleaning out a closet. Now that it's cleared out, what would you like to fill the space with?

You can choose the same affirmation/mantra each time or switch it up depending on what you just released. I am safe, I am in action, I am awesome, I am brave, I am worthy. I am at peace. I am joyous. We're going to talk about affirmations in just a bit, so you should develop plenty of experience with them to make this final piece feel natural.

ALARM Method Summary

Use this ALARM method anytime to deal with negative and lower vibration emotions on the spot. Make sure as you swipe down each arm (unpack) that you declare the release of that feeling, unprocessed emotion, or sabotage belief and replace it with a new mantra.

AWARENESS: Notice the feeling you are having or the feeling the belief has caused.

LOCATE: Find where it is in the body.

ASK: Ask yourself, "When have I felt this before?"

RELEASE: Allow the feeling to expand and unpack.

MANTRA: Speak what you would like to feel/believe.

Muscle Testing

There are many ways to discover and then release unprocessed emotions—meditation, tuning forks, acupuncture, Jin Shin Jyutsu acupressure, and guided visualizations to name a few. Another powerful method that anyone can use is muscle testing and it's easy to learn. Simply put, muscle testing is a safe, natural method of analyzing the body's needs using the body's reflexes. Muscle testing is biofeedback from the body.

Remember we talked about how everyone and everything is made up of energy? This is a way to tap into the body's energetic field—a way to speak to the subconscious. Manual muscle testing has been used for over 60 years by doctors and physical therapists to evaluate muscle function. In the 1960s, Dr. George Goodheart used muscle testing to diagnose meridian, nerve, and muscle energy function and connections. More than just a diagnostic procedure, his discoveries led to the creation of a new system of assessment and healing that we know as applied kinesiology.

I've been using muscle testing for years to determine which supplements work best for me and with other simple "yes/no" questions. Additionally, with previous hands-on healing work, I learned how to connect with clients over distance sessions.

I wanted to learn more about using this tool to assist clients in releasing sabotage beliefs, so I read everything I could get my hands on, practicing on myself for hours. What I discovered was not only did muscle testing work for identifying sabotage beliefs but I could muscle test on behalf of my clients.

While exploring the processes of identifying and releasing sabotage behaviors, I hit gold when I discovered that Dr. Bradley Nelson, author of, "The Emotion Code," uses muscle testing to identify unprocessed emotions. He spent decades studying and crafting a method that helps people identify and release what he calls *trapped emotions.* If you want to geek out on an amazing book around emotions, this has all the details from a researcher's perspective.

Muscle testing can be used for communicating directly with the body and the subconscious. This is a skill that can come in super handy for choosing supplements, books to read, deciphering truth in a statement or situation, grocery shopping choices, and of course, for our purposes here, identifying sabotage beliefs, unprocessed emotions, and limiting setpoints.

"How the body responds can give us clues on what is stuck and what needs to heal."

In addition to assessing the strength of an individual muscle's response, we can assess the body's energetic response to questions. Biochemical, electromagnetic, physical, emotional, and mental responses all have an impact on the body's energy field and subsequently register on the nervous system, which will affect muscle response. How the body responds can give us clues on what is stuck and what needs to heal.

There was a time when I was dealing with a lot of health problems. I was taking a lot of supplements but felt exhausted all of the time. I connected with a naturopath who practiced out of Atlanta. I flew down to see her and we did many tests including bloodwork. We found through muscle testing I was allergic to some of the supplements I had been taking plus a few other foods my body didn't like that I thought were healthy. After that, I muscle-tested everything I could.

How to Muscle Test

There are many ways to muscle test, everything from snapping your fingers, moving your hand across a surface, using a pendulum, and many more. The sway test (explained below) is my favorite for its simplicity, but feel free to search for the way that works best for you. You can find additional ways to muscle test at my website jenniepotter.com.

Sway Test

Stand up tall with your feet pointing directly forward, hip-width apart. Make sure they're not turned slightly in or out. Relax your body and keep your arms down by your side. Notice how you sway ever so slightly even as you stand still. To begin, you need to ask a foundational question to check for accuracy.

- Speak your correct name out loud. My name is

  _____.

- Now tune into the movement of your body.

- Speak a false name out loud. My name is

  _____.

Again, tune into the movement of your body. Think about it this way, you lean into and towards truth positivity, and you fall away from negativity and deceit. At this moment, look for which way your body sways.

Now that you are tuned in to your body's movement, you can ask "yes/no" questions to continue using the sway test. Be mindful of the response of your body to each statement. You should feel yourself gently pulled forward for a correct response, a "yes" or pushed back indicating it's not true or your body is not in resonance with that, which would be a "no" response.

For example:

Am I still holding onto anger about my sister's passing?

If you get a "yes," then you can continue to ask deeper, more specific questions.

Things to be Aware Of

You can also apply muscle testing to other types of healing. In the following section, you can use the list of emotions and common sabotage beliefs to see if you have anything to release in those areas.

Muscle test to see if you have any unprocessed emotions and release them systematically as you go through the list. Use the unpacking movement in the ALARM method to release. It's always powerful to close out any release with a powerful mantra/affirmation. As you release low vibration emotions and beliefs you can use new mantras to fill your energetic space with a higher vibration.

Several variables can affect muscle testing results. It is important to create your base test and use "yes or no" questions. Keeping a neutral mind is ideal. Don't wear a hat, it seems to skew the results. Being hydrated is also important as hydration can affect the body's ability to optimally conduct accurate nervous system feedback.

Other possible interferences could be drugs, alcohol, reaction to diet, stress, fatigue, blood sugar, etc. Always start with your base test and go from there so you know you are getting an accurate reading. The best example is using your real and then a false name.

Additionally, I always begin my sessions for myself and when working with clients by setting an intention for the highest good to come of the session. I include prayer and ask God for assistance. Although this is not a necessary step for muscle testing, it has become part of my process.

The work feels nothing short of miraculous. I am grateful to God for the healing that occurs and the gift of muscle testing to communicate with our subconscious and our bodies so that we may clear what could be holding us back.

Your UPE Score

I promised that we'd talk about determining your UPE score (Unprocessed Emotion Score) and now we're ready. How? You can simply muscle test to discover this number as well. I muscle-tested for unprocessed emotions and *bingo*. I had them. 496 of them to be exact.

To determine your UPE, simply start by asking, "Do I have more than 200 unprocessed emotions?" If you sense a no, then ask, "Is it more than 100?" If you get a yes, then ask again, "Is it more than 150?" Continue to ask until you land on the number. On average my adult clients tend to have around 200 though I have seen as few as five and as many as 1,906.

To date, I have helped people release thousands of emotions. I'd love to hear from you how many you released. Post your UPE score and how many emotions you have released to date using the hashtag #UPEscore on social media!

After you feel you have mastered muscle testing, you can go through the following list of emotions to see if you have that emotion stuck somewhere from a past event. You can also use muscle testing to see if you cleared the emotion or not.

This may be the missing piece for you. It was for me. After I released all of my trapped emotions, I saw a dramatic change in the way I showed up daily. I was less reactive, more loving, more me, more focused, and had increased empathy for myself and others. I noticed more clearly what was mine and, more importantly, what was not. I stopped procrastinating, stopped getting migraines, gained back my energy, and faced the day differently. I started asking my clients if we could try identifying trapped emotions in the same way we had been identifying sabotage beliefs.

See my list of the most common low vibration emotions which come up and are released during the session.

powerlessness	discouragement	unappreciated
unworthiness	disappointment	overwhelm
depression	vulnerability	frustration
insecurity	humiliation	irritation
anxiety	unsupported	impatience
despair	trauma/shock	pessimism
grief	jealousy	boredom
shame	blame	doubt
pride	anger	guilt
worry	rage	

Releasing Sabotage Beliefs

Look at the following list of common sabotage beliefs on the following page (also known as limiting beliefs or false beliefs) and muscle test the following list. If you still have not mastered muscle testing, you can use the ALARM method and notice where you feel each statement. If you are unsure of any, mark them as a "yes."

If you are using muscle testing, you can test each statement with the question, "Do I have this limiting belief?"

Common Sabotage Beliefs

☐ I am worthless

☐ I am ugly

☐ The world is unsafe

☐ I don't deserve love

☐ I'll never be loved

☐ I hate myself

☐ I don't have control

☐ I don't deserve forgiveness

☐ I'm not worthy of respect

☐ I'm stuck

☐ I'm trapped

☐ I destroy everything

☐ I'm all alone

☐ I'll never be accepted

☐ I'm not enough

☐ I'm broken/unfixable

☐ There's not enough

☐ There's not enough time

☐ I'm an imposter

☐ I'm dangerous

☐ I'm out of control

☐ I'm a mess

☐ I'm stupid

☐ Everything is dangerous/scary

☐ I shouldn't exist

☐ I don't belong

☐ I'll never catch up/I'm behind

☐ There's no point in trying

☐ I never win

☐ I'm not important

☐ I'm too old

☐ Everyone's needs are more important than mine

☐ Growth is painful

☐ Wealth is hard

☐ Money is bad

☐ I have to earn love

☐ I'm weak

☐ I'm not a priority

☐ People will betray me

☐ Making money is stressful

☐ I can't have it all

☐ If I shine, others get hurt

After you have identified your sabotage beliefs, you can release them with the unpacking method. This is three sweeping movements, shoulder to wrist, on each arm. Include a new mantra that is the opposite of the sabotage belief you are releasing. For example, say the sabotage belief is, *I'll never be accepted.* Unpack that with six sweeping movements.

As a bonus, you can do the unpacking movement again and replace it with a new mantra, such as, I am always accepted.

Now, reset your filter to search for proof of what you want to see. In the example of "I am accepted," you could grab a pen and paper and brainstorm all of the ways you are accepted. Where are the areas you are included and welcome? You want to reset your filter to notice and let in where you are accepted.

Here is an overview of the process at a glance:

The Process at-a-Glance*

☐ 1. Use muscle testing to identify or confirm unprocessed emotions and sabotage beliefs.

☐ 2. Use the unpacking method to release what you find.

☐ 3. Use the unpacking method to replace those with a new mantra.

☐ 4. Muscle test to see if the emotion/sabotage belief was released.

*Alternatively, you can also use the ALARM method to identify and release.

Sabotage Setpoints

Once you have been through the process of releasing all of your unprocessed emotions and sabotage beliefs (ideally bringing your UPE score down to zero), you can turn your attention to the next piece in the puzzle which is sabotage setpoints.

What are setpoints? Setpoints are limits or ceilings that we can intentionally or unintentionally set around what we believe is possible. This includes categories such as happiness, relationship contentedness, finances, physical health, spirituality, success, career, etc.

The best example I can give of a classic setpoint is metabolic setpoints.

Have you ever been on a diet and reached a number on the scale that you just can't seem to get below, no matter how hard you try? Or you lose 10 pounds, only to gain it right back?

This is because your body will adjust its metabolic burn rate and hold on to the weight to get back into what it believes is the correct number or *balance*. In this case, the body chooses a weight set point. That is the point of balance and homeostasis. To change your weight successfully, up or down, you need to reset this setpoint.

- Do you have a sabotage set point for how much money you make?
- How happy you will allow yourself to be?
- How much praise you will accept?
- How much success is okay for you?

In his book, "The Big Leap," Gay Hendricks says, "Each of us has an inner thermostat setting that determines how much love, success, and creativity we allow ourselves to enjoy. When we exceed our inner thermostat setting, we will often do something to sabotage ourselves, causing us to drop back into the old, familiar zone where we feel secure."

"All sabotage setpoints are self-imposed limits unintentionally set through life experiences or observations."

Maybe you have had a period where "everything seems too good to be true." Or, every time your financial life is going exceedingly well, you notice your relationships start to fall apart. Maybe you notice that after hitting a big goal like paying off some debt, you find something else you *have to* go into debt for. Or you drop that weight, then stop exercising and start eating ice cream as soon as you notice the progress. Maybe you get sick when an opportunity to change your life arises, or something you have to do interrupts the chance to change your life. Or, after earning an award or promotion you start showing up late, stop producing, and start dropping the ball.

All sabotage setpoints are self-imposed limits unintentionally set through life experiences or observations.

The triggers for these sabotage setpoints are often either unprocessed emotions or sabotage beliefs. As you release those, you will notice it is easier to identify and reset your setpoints.

Gay Hendricks describes these setpoints as Upper Limits. One of the most common culprits he names is the "crime of outshining." He describes it in the following way:

"The unconscious mantra of the outshining barrier goes like this:

I must not expand to my full success, because if I did, I would outshine (name of person) and make him or her look or feel bad."

When I was exploring and discovering setpoints, I found this one locked in me from a young age. I had a vivid memory of my brother and me handing over our report cards to my father. I excelled at school and was a shy and well-behaved kid. My brother was always getting into trouble, couldn't sit still, and was curious about everything. As I received praise and my brother received the opposite, I remember feeling sick. I felt like it was my fault he was in trouble. If I hadn't done so well, maybe it wouldn't have been bad for him. I understood at that moment that when I shine it's not good for others. I locked in this core belief: When I shine, others get hurt. And that's how my dimmer switch was born.

So how did this affect me growing up?

I dimmed my light, shining a little but never too much. I was good at lifting others up and stepping back. I used to always say I was a great co-pilot, right-hand man, a passenger, not a driver. I didn't like competing or feel comfortable winning games. If you played Monopoly with me and were on the losing side, there was no need to worry because I'd give you my money, so we could keep playing and no one would lose. Later in life, it affected me in bigger ways.

A few years ago, I won a distributor of the year award in my company. It was an award I had dreamed of, visualized, and spoken to in the mirror thousands of times. When I heard my name called to the stage, I started to cry. My dreams had come to fruition—I was living my best life. To hit this goal, I worked tirelessly and consistently. I did the things necessary to be successful, which for me were doing Facebook Lives, posting on social media, inviting people to look at my business, making presentations, etc.

That evening, an hour after I received the award, and I was still sky high, someone in the company, whom I deeply respected and looked up to, walked over to me and hugged me. She whispered in my ear, "Congratulations honey! You know, *so and so* (she named a fellow distributor) is crying in her hotel room right now because she didn't get the award, right?" And with that, she walked away.

Wham!

Gut punch.

Just like that, I was down. Just like that, I felt sick. That old familiar feeling. *When I shine others get hurt.* Keep in mind this is hindsight. The belief was triggered but I didn't know that at the time. What I knew was, I was feeling on top of the world one moment and the next moment, I was feeling small and sick.

The next day, I did not do a Facebook Live video. That next week, I did no networking, and in the following weeks, I stopped doing all the things that had earned me the award in the first place. I stopped showing up, and it was a total mystery to me.

I kept wondering, what was wrong with me? Why don't I feel like building my business? Why don't I feel self-motivated anymore?

I hit my success setpoint. The award, the comment, and the success triggered my sabotage setpoint: my belief that it's not safe to shine, not safe to succeed. The belief that "others get hurt when I shine" lit up and just like that, the subconscious in its lightning-fast way took over and I self-sabotaged.

Sabotage Setpoint Triggers

A few areas I have uncovered that have measurable setpoints include:

- Relationships (friendships, significant other)
- Career
- Financial
- Family (children, parents, siblings)
- Health
- Spiritual connection
- Emotional health
- Having it all

I can only be this happy, have this much money, have this much praise, be this healthy, etc.

Have you ever noticed that you always earn around the same amount of money no matter the company or job title? That you come into some extra money only to have almost the same amount go out unexpectedly? If that is you, you may have a financial setpoint; a place your subconscious deems acceptable, based on previous life experience.

WENDY'S STORY

My client Wendy was like this. She and her husband had an extremely successful business over a decade ago and had built a powerful name in the community. They were passionate about their work and in some ways, had defied the odds and were earning a monthly income beyond their dreams. But then out of the blue, a family member close to them, one they had always trusted, betrayed them and destroyed their name and income. They had to declare bankruptcy, move back in with their parents, and start all over again. They worked hard day and night with very little success. They felt a quiet "told you so" from the naysayers and took years to recover from the blow.

When they started over, their belief in their financial abilities was very low, their set point just covered their bills, and they were having to dip into their savings.

As Wendy and I began to work together, we identified the fear of success, which was tied to the previous pain of betrayal and loss. We released unprocessed emotions, let go of sabotage beliefs and reset her financial setpoint.

When we began our work together, we determined Wendy had 102 unprocessed emotions. She was full of anger, resentment, and feelings of betrayal. She experienced a high level of procrastination on any task she attempted towards making the business work—her days were filled with little to no action and a lot of unhappiness with herself. However, in only four sessions she released those emotions and rediscovered her passion for the business. She no longer aches with loss, but rather finds joy in her family business. Within a couple of months of releasing her unprocessed emotions and resetting her sabotage setpoints, Wendy and her husband experienced their most successful month in 20 years, doubling their normal sales from the business.

Resetting Sabotage Setpoints

S o how do we assess, release, and reset sabotage setpoints? As I just mentioned, sabotage setpoints are the limits (ceilings) that we intentionally or unintentionally set around what we believe is possible. This includes categories such as happiness, having it all, relationship contentedness, finances, physical health, spirituality, success, career, etc. Please keep in mind that through trial and error, I have discovered this works best when you have already completely cleared your UPE score and your sabotage beliefs.

As a coach and someone who works with clients using these techniques, the most frequently requested sessions I get are for resetting physical weight and financial setpoints. The best part (and why I wrote this book) is you can absolutely do this on your own.

On the following page is a chart that you can use in conjunction with muscle testing to check your "setpoint" number out of 99. This will give you an idea of how much you need to improve in each category, 99 being your highest score.

This might feel like magic, but it's merely shifting your mind and energy to "reset" and accept a new level in whichever category you choose.

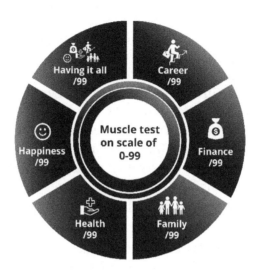

The chart is useful for your overall scale.

You can also reset specific numbers such as metabolic setpoints and financial ceilings you can't seem to break through.

Use the "unpacking" movement we discussed earlier to reset your sabotage setpoint. Do this movement three times, then muscle test to see if it is reset. As you work on shifting your categories, you can also pick a specific topic and number and work with it.

This chart is a suggestion of categories, but there are many subjects you can use this exercise with. Metabolic setpoints, personal growth, savings, etc. The point is, you can choose your categories, these are just to get you started.

As I write this, I am resetting my weight setpoint, slowly and steadily. I spent the majority of my life around 150 pounds. This was a weight I felt comfortable at.

A couple of years ago with attention to my exercise, drinking water, and intermittent fasting, I maintained about 145 pounds and felt strong and happy with my size and fitness level.

There was one problem. Each time I would dive into a fitness program to strengthen my core, I would have severe pain (what I call my "cyst" pain) that would flare up. It's a pain that had put me in and out of the hospital for 20 years. I was super frustrated. When I went to the hospital (always sure something had burst or gone wrong), they would say it was probably just a cyst, give me morphine, and send me home. I stopped going to the emergency room because I figured if they weren't going to do anything to help me heal I could suffer through the pain at home.

Then one day I went to see a chiropractor about something else. He had all the latest X-ray machines and was super thorough. When he came out to show me the results he looked upset. He said he couldn't work on me because he had found a mass in my abdominal region. He had never seen anything like it and said I should see my doctor immediately. The short version of a very long story is they set up surgery to remove the mass. There were unexpected complications and it ended up being a 6-hour surgery instead of the originally planned 20-minute procedure.

For about a week, I couldn't get out of my bed without assistance, my husband had to carry me to the washroom. I was very weak and exhausted. I stopped any kind of exercise for at least 6 months. I felt a bit depressed. I ate differently and my hormones were out of whack. The result? I gained 30 pounds—and over the next year and a half, nothing I did would release it. If you have ever had extra weight on you that won't budge you understand my frustration. I had never struggled with weight before.

My old set point sat between 145–150 pounds. My new set point? Stuck at 180. For 18 months, no movement. Then I tried a reset.

At first, I tried to reset it back to 145 from 180. It did not stick. Then I tried increments and it started to work better. For some people, larger increments work. For others (like me) it is one pound at a time. As I write this I have been releasing about 1 pound a week, slow and steady. I reset to 179, then 178, 177, etc. This works. I changed nothing else, have released 10 pounds, and am still dropping.

So, with your new muscle testing abilities, you can reset your weight set point. First, ask the question, "Is my weight set point higher than or lower than ___?"

Then the next question is, can I reset to (put in your desired healthy weight)?

When I first started, this is what day one looked like. I muscle tested:

Is my weight set point 180? *I received a "yes."*

- Can I reset to 145? *I received a no.*
- Can I reset to 155? *No again.*
- Can I reset to 165? *Another no.*
- Can I reset to 175? *Still no.*
- Can I reset to 179? *Finally, I got a yes.*

I do this weekly. You can play around with this, do it daily, every other day, etc. See what is a fit for you. You can even ask. Can I reset in one day, two days, or three days, etc.?

What about financial setpoints?

This question varies from person to person and also depends on how you think about and measure your income. I work with salespeople who think in terms of weeks, months, quarters, or years.

One of my clients, Chris, who felt stuck at $325,000 a year, knew it was just a mindset thing but could not push past the setpoint of this amount. After we released all of his unprocessed emotions and many sabotage beliefs around money, we reset to the next setpoint that he was open to embracing. Ultimately, $500,000 was the number. That week after the reset, Chris was offered a signing bonus of $175,000 to join a different brokerage.

When you think about your income, what is the first number that comes to mind? Imagine if you could shift your unseen financial blocks. You can. First, determine your financial setpoint (weekly, monthly, yearly) whatever is the most common way you think about your income.

Next through muscle testing determine your new setpoint. This is usually a stretch but not a strain and can go up incrementally, too. Notice how money flows to you in new ways. Unexpected money in the mail. New business opportunities. Owed money flows back to you.

Celebrate every dollar as if it is a million. Get into the vibration of abundance. Shift your financial setpoint and shift your income.

There are endless categories of set points. Maybe you have a team of 100 people, and you would like a team of 1,000 or more. Maybe you would like to have additional income streams or need a certain amount of money to be debt free. Maybe you want to sell above a certain number of units like books sold, or products bought. Maybe you have a certain setpoint with followers on your social media accounts.

Check out the chart to be your guide but don't be afraid to set your own categories. The options are endless. Muscle test to see if you have a set point, then reset it.

It's All About Vibration

We discussed earlier in the book that setpoints, emotions, and beliefs all have a vibration of their own—a frequency. If yours are stuck and resonating at a lower vibration, then they lower *your* vibration. So, you must understand not only how you can release trapped vibrations but also how you can raise your vibration. Why is this important?

You attract your vibe, plain and simple.

Your vibe is your tribe, your finances, your opportunities, your health, your... *everything!*

The most common ways taught to change your vibration are the following vibrational adjusters:

1. *Affirmations*
2. *Daily gratitude*
3. *Visualizations*

Before you roll your eyes and say, these again? Read on.

I know everyone writes about gratitude, "I AM" statements, and visualization. So, you've likely read this before but there is a reason this stuff is in every single self-help book you read.

It works.

It's possible you didn't roll your eyes and instead might be feeling a little optimistic here, knowing you are generally a positive person with pretty good thoughts. And you may already practice these things and have a daily routine down.

Affirmations. *Check.*

Gratitude. *Check.*

Visualizations. *Check.*

Perhaps you're scratching your head wondering why all the self-help books speak to attracting what you want, and you haven't seen any noticeable success. Or things are still coming slow or not at all. Maybe you feel that there is an invisible block, and no matter how hard you try, you can't get out of your own way.

Have you had the experience that affirmations don't change your life quickly? Well, hold on tight because if you have released the unprocessed emotions or are working on letting them go, things are about to speed up.

"Affirmations can change your circumstances, your vibration, and what you attract into your life."

For the reader who doesn't know what affirmations are, they are basically *"I am..."* statements said in the present tense where you fill in the blank with something you desire. Done regularly and correctly, affirmations can change your circumstances, your vibration, and what you attract into your life.

The first time I ever did affirmations to manifest what I wanted, I was a child. I didn't know how powerful I was and actually scared myself.

My mom was away on a girls' hiking trip and my dad was tasked to take care of my brother and me. I was 7 years old, and my brother was 9. He made us blueberry pancakes which was extra fun because he rarely cooked. I didn't want to go to school and wanted to hang out with him instead. I told him I was feeling sick and thought I should stay home. My Dad didn't believe me (for good reason, I wasn't sick) and told me I was fine and to get my backpack because it was time to go to school.

My 7-year-old brain was frustrated, a little shocked, and even hurt that he didn't believe me! So, I decided I was sick. I said over and over, "Dad, please, I don't feel well, I don't want to go to school." He lovingly put my backpack on me (fully reading the situation correctly) and sent me out the door to walk to school with my brother.

All the way to school I stuck to my guns. *I don't feel good, I feel sick, I want to throw up.* And for the entire walk, I affirmed to my brother repeatedly that I was sick. When we got to school, I walked into class, sat down at my desk, and threw up all of my blueberry pancakes.

They called my dad, and he came and picked me up. I will never forget the guilt showing on his face and the guilt and confusion I felt inside, too. I got to spend the day with Dad. I also remember understanding that I had made myself sick. I never lied about how I was feeling again.

Okay, so chances are you don't want to make yourself sick but perhaps you have a different goal?

How do you go about affirmations more intentionally?

How to do Affirmations

Look into the mirror and speak out loud all of the things, experiences, and achievements you want in your life as if they have *already happened.* Do this every single day, multiple times a day (think blueberry pancakes) if possible. Slowly or quickly (depending upon your vibration), you'll attract what you are affirming into your life.

Examples:

- *I am living my best life.*
- *I am a best-selling published author.*
- *I am a top earner.*
- *I make millions with ease.*
- *I love my new title.*
- *I love my purpose.*
- *I am attracting money in unexpected ways.*
- *I am favored.*
- *I attract new opportunities.*
- *I attract new customers.*

Sounds simple right? Have you tried this, and it didn't work? I can truly say that affirmations changed my life, but it took over a decade! It felt like I was running chest-deep in water instead of running on the sand or even on the sidewalk.

Had I known then what I know now, I believe I could have changed the trajectory of my life much sooner. I would have been on the sidewalk much faster.

Where was I when I discovered affirmations? I remember exactly where I was. I wasn't running chest-deep in water, but rather was drowning in a sea of self-loathing, blame, guilt, and brokenness.

It was 2006. These were the sabotage years. I was standing in front of the mirror in my new apartment. Broken. Crushed. Single. Seeing nothing but ugliness as I stared in the mirror. Willing myself to say the words. Willing myself to stop thinking the ugly thoughts like, "Who would ever want you? You're ugly, you're dirty, you are less, you are unlovable, you are unfixable, used up, old, lost, and wrong..."

I was in agony and wanted so much more.

There was this tiny seed of hope in me, a grain of possibility... what if I could be more? Could I be fixed, healed, beautiful? There was a time when I was so full of hope. When I dreamt of being a healer, writer, and speaker—a time when I believed.

Where had that Jennie gone?

At that moment, as I stared in the mirror, all I had was the sleeping bag on the floor behind me, a couple of pots and pans in the kitchen, a shower curtain, and some personal belongings. I had taken almost nothing with me when I left the darkness and the twisted decade of self-sabotage. I found myself here, relieved, depressed, and alone.

"Shift your vibration and feel better and attract better."

The solitude that brought safety also exposed the reality of my very lonely situation. I hated myself and what I had done. What I had become. I hated what I had endured for the last decade and what I had accepted for the last 10 years of my life. I also knew there was no one to blame but me. I had lost myself. Yet there I was. Standing in front of the mirror. Broken and alone, willing myself to take that first step toward a new vision, a new version of me. Willing myself to be found.

That day marked the day when everything changed. You see, I had prayed for help and almost immediately I connected with a healer. She told me to do something remarkably simple. Something I had never heard of. She said, "Stand in front of the mirror, look yourself in the eye, and tell yourself three affirmations daily. In the present. In the now."

So, I chose:

I am worthy of love.

I am beautiful.

I love myself.

That was the beginning of my journey to end my self-sabotage. No simple task. No turning back.

Those first days I felt like a fraud. I could not even look myself in the eye. But I did it. Every day. *I am worthy of love. I am beautiful. I love myself. I am worthy of love. I am beautiful. I love myself,* over and over and over. Slowly but surely my life began to shift. Years later, I found and married the love of my life and got two beautiful stepkids. I could look myself in the eye with joy and gratitude for my beauty (inside and out) and I knew I loved myself fully and completely.

It's no lie when I tell you this took over a decade of some pretty diligent speaking to the mirror.

Affirmations work and I discovered they work best with praise, and gratitude (high vibrations) but the process can take a while for some people. Why? Why is it so quick for some and so slow for others? What if there is a missing piece you have been sort of aware of but can't quite release? What if you aren't sure if you are doing it right?

One of the tough things about manifesting is changing how we *feel.* We do affirmations to shift our thoughts, our thoughts lead to feelings, and then those feelings affect our behavior. All of this leads to what we see—opportunity versus trapped, lucky versus unlucky, or broke versus rich.

Shift your vibration and feel better and attract better.

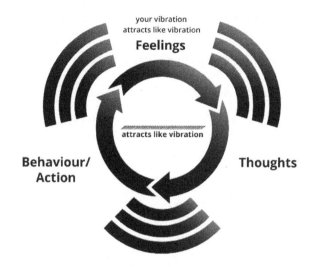

But what if you feel broke? You desperately need money to pay a bill, purchase something, go somewhere, bless someone, or do a renovation. How do we change that vibe? Here's my best affirmation hack for when you are feeling broke plus a couple of others, too.

Affirmation Hack: *When You Feel Broke*

When you are feeling broke, ask yourself, *what am I rich in?*

Then notice it, declare it, dance about it, and celebrate it!

Are you rich in dishes?

Glassware?

Blades of grass?

Water?

T-shirts?

Quarters?

Furniture?

Doohickies?

Air to breathe?

Declare it! Speak it out! *I am rich in dishes!*

Here are two more of my favorite hacks for getting beyond what might be sabotaging your affirmations:

Affirmation Hack: *I Wonder…*

If you speak out your affirmation and immediately feel what I call a "kickback" (the voice in your head that says, *yeah right,* followed by a sick feeling in the pit of your stomach), try this.

Let's say your affirmation is, *"I am earning $50,000 per month."* The dollar amount is whatever *you* want; it could be $5,000 or $500,000, it's up to you!

Now instead of saying, "I am earning $50,000 a month," you say, "I wonder what it would feel like to earn $50,000 a month?"

Your brain will search for the answer. *Et Voila!* You are on your way to a new vibe!

Affirmation Hack: *Mix It Up*

The main reason people get frustrated with affirmations is they feel like they are lying to themselves. One approach is to affirm what you *already* have, along with what you are wanting to attract.

For example:

- I am grateful for my amazing closet that looks professionally organized! (That's one you don't have.)
- I am excited about the checks coming in the mail. (You already have this.)
- A steady job (You already have this.)
- I got the promotion at work (Looking forward to this.)

- I am worthy of love (isn't everyone?)
- I am powerful (deep down we all have untapped power.)
- I am courageous (maybe you haven't been yet, but...)

Merge what *is* with what *could* be, and watch your vibe change, then watch your life change!

Bonus Power Up!

Use the unpacking movement and speak out your affirmation. Have the intention that you are stepping into that new affirmation.

Example: Say, "I am abundant," (three times) while sweeping down the arm from shoulder to wrist with the other hand. Then alternate. Do this 3-6 times.

Power of Gratitude

Maybe instead of, or in addition to affirmations, you have focused on daily gratitude. Many of my clients tell me they are grateful for everything they have, and in the same breath, they tell me what they don't have, what they can't seem to manifest, where they are stuck, and what's wrong. They tell me what they are not grateful for and what they haven't created.

Herein lies the problem.

Of course, gratitude is being grateful for what you have. But if you are doing gratitude correctly, you are grateful for the lottery *you have not yet won* as if you have already won it. It is a straightforward way of changing your physical vibration, the same way you do affirmations: *as if it already happened.*

Five years ago, my husband and I saw a house on the market that was dreamy in structure and layout. It had the perfect number of bedrooms for us and the kids, plus an office for me. The kids' space was completely separate from ours and as they had moved into their teenage years, this was ideal for them and us. It was soundproof, which I loved for my writing, webinars, and coaching calls. It also had a barn with a bonus space for our gym equipment and four bays for cars. (My hubby collects old Toyota trucks, fixes them, and sells them so the extra parking would be dreamy.) It was almost a couple of acres and had a beautiful stone wall, it was well built, and it was my husband's dream home. The kids loved it, too. There was only one problem. Although its flooring was in perfect shape, it was not aesthetically pleasing, given the 3,000 square feet of orange and pink carpet and hospital-looking linoleum.

The kitchen counters were forest green; the fridge was an old-school black with fake wood paneling. It was perfectly preserved and 30 years behind the times.

But the moment we all walked in, it felt like home. I could even live with the outdatedness—except for that darn carpet. So, we made a deal. It was a stretch at the time but manageable. We decided to borrow enough so that we could buy the house and put in new floors before we moved in.

Three days before we closed on the deal, the bank called. They wanted a bigger down payment or would not approve the mortgage they had already preapproved. We scrambled and made it happen. We put our dreams for the floors on hold and moved into the pink and orange carpeted home. *Did I mention my husband loved the floors?* He has always maintained function over fashion, and I knew in my heart it was fine but deep down every day, felt this frustration that I hadn't manifested the floors I wanted.

After two years, I had kind of gotten used to the floors and was a little less attached to changing them. Who were they for anyway? What on earth do I need hardwood for? We barely entertain. We had priced them out, and there were so many other things we would prefer to spend our money on that I wasn't sure it would ever happen.

Then one day it clicked.

I had manifested so many things in my life, a loving husband, an amazing career where I got to work from home, a healthy family, an SUV I loved to drive, travel with my company, opportunities to speak, and a residual income.

Why not floors?

So, I started to speak gratitude to them... I LOVED those floors! I danced on them, sang to them, and was grateful for every step I took. I was grateful for the floors I had. I admired their perfect condition and I made it a daily mission to find things I was grateful for as I walked through the house. I said nothing to my husband. And guess what? Two things happened. I started loving the floors *for real* and we came into some money unexpectedly which my husband out of the blue suggested we use for new floors.

"When we are grateful, we uplevel and raise our vibration."

After only four months of me loving and being grateful for those floors, we were walking on the hardwood of our dreams. We still love the floors and are grateful for them. They transformed our home. It was a small thing but a huge thing. I still feel gratitude with every step I take.

The flooring guys told us we needed to get a new fridge, that the old one would damage the new hardwood, so the kids got a fun fridge downstairs for their stuff, and I danced my way out of the kitchen to update the ugly wood-paneled fridge. Danced. Next, I did it for the countertops and am currently working on the bathrooms.

I share this story because it was my gratitude that changed everything. As soon as I learned to stop hating the floors, stopped frowning at the fridge and countertops, and started appreciating and being grateful for what was, *everything changed.*

When we are grateful, we uplevel and raise our vibration. When we are grateful, we are open to receiving. With gratitude comes blessings.

Here are a few more of my go-to "gratitude hacks."

Gratitude Hack: *Raising Hallelujah*

For the faith-filled individual, this is a power-packed daily routine. Include God in your gratitude. Using the acronym P.A.T.H. you can speak out your gratitude in the following way:

Pray—heartfelt prayer declaring what is on your heart

Affirm—affirmation that all is well and has come to fruition.

Thank—giving gratitude for all you have and all that is coming.

Hallelujah/praise—praising God for all your blessings, answered prayers, and unanswered prayers.

Even if your beliefs do not exactly fit this exercise, spending time in reflection, affirming, thanking, and giving praise for all life has brought you, is incredibly powerful.

Gratitude Hack: *Write it Out*

Write out ten things you are grateful for each morning, then speak it out loud, then spend a few minutes reflecting on the things you are grateful for. You can also add in a gratitude walk and notice everything you are grateful for!

Gratitude Hack: *Gratitude for Others*

Message one person daily for 30 days and tell them why you are grateful for them in your life.

Be authentic. Why are you grateful specifically for them? What makes them unique? Really spend time thinking about how that person has blessed you. These can be people you know well (friends, family members, colleagues, or team members) and also the author of a book you love, a podcaster or influencer you enjoy following online, or a speaker who inspired you. Send them a message.

Visualization

The final piece of the vibrational power trio is visualization. I didn't practice visualization for years. It wasn't my natural fallback (affirmations were within my comfort zone, visualization was not), and so I would gloss over the suggestion to visualize with every self-help book I read.

I wish I had discovered sooner *why* visualization works. It works in the same kind of way that the computer remembers my daughter's email instead of mine. Because just like the computer, we are "dumb-smart" and can use this "dumb-smart" to our advantage.

What do I mean?

Have you ever watched a horror movie and been legitimately scared—and gone to bed with the lights on? Is that smart? You *know* it's not real.

Ever watch a romance and cry when they reunite at the end? Ever grip the edge of your seat at a movie theatre wondering if the main character will live? You know it's not real but you feel like it is.

Your brain, as miraculous as it is, *does not know the difference between real life and the screen.* Your brain is "dumb-smart." It does not know the difference between what you visualize and what you see with your eyes.

Remember earlier we talked about the tractor beam? When you visualize something you want as if you have it, the brain thinks *you have this*, your vibration shifts upwards and you start pulling in what you already have.

You are imagining bills paid with ease. Your book published or that promotion. *(You can message me if you bought this on Amazon or at the airport! I envisioned you buying it before you did.)*

The brain doesn't know your visualization isn't real and hasn't happened yet. And what's even better? You start to vibrate at a level of receiving what you are thinking about and focusing on. Watching a lot of crime movies? Violent video games? Sad stories on the news? What are you imagining while you are driving? What you should have said to that mean co-worker or the idea of making millions with ease? It matters.

"Are you addicted to thinking about bad outcomes? Worst case scenarios?"

What are you thinking about as you fall asleep? Losing everything or standing on stage inspiring millions? A future dinner party going horribly wrong or the best ever? Opportunities coming your way? Being mentored by someone you could never imagine being in the same room with? Mentoring thousands of others to change their lives? Living in the house of your dreams? Healing or hurting? Scarcity or abundance?

Are you addicted to thinking about bad outcomes? Worst case scenarios?

Most people visualize every day... *but* they don't do it with intention. Most people spend their energy and time thinking about what they don't want, tractor beaming in what they don't want, and scratching their heads about why they stay in the same old patterns year after year.

Sabotaging Your Good Vibrations

I once used visualizations and affirmations to win a car in Las Vegas. I was in my late 20s (these were still my self-sabotage days) but was starting to see a faint light in the distance.

I owed a lot of money at the time and was stressed out by my lack of income and ever-increasing debt. My credit card was over the limit—I owed student loans and other money I had no idea how I was going to pay off.

I decided to manifest the money I needed to pay off my debt. I had what I owed down to the penny. If my memory is correct, it was $17,277.78.

I'd heard that if you sat down and focused intently on an exact number each day that you could manifest it. So, every morning for three weeks, I focused intently on that amount. I affirmed that the amount appeared easily for me and visualized being excited about it. I imagined paying off my debt. I imagined the relief.

After about three weeks, an unexpected opportunity to go to Vegas popped up. I liked playing blackjack and thought for sure this was how I was going to pay off my debt. I played a bunch of hands and didn't win. I played slot machines, didn't win, and was disappointed that my visualizations had not worked.

But there was this drawing that the casino was having to win a car. Any time a player got the same suit blackjack, they would get an entry for the drawing. Just as I was leaving to fly back home, I remembered I had won a draw ticket. I filled it out quickly and threw it in the huge clear plastic box along with thousands of other entries.

About a month later, I received a call from the casino—I won. I won a sixty-thousand-dollar car! All I had to do was fly down to Las Vegas, pick it up, and drive it home. But I live in Canada and when you bring a car over the border (no matter how you got it), you have to pay a hefty amount of taxes.

After a few phone calls, I realized I would need money to get to Vegas (did I mention I was broke?) plus approximately $10,000 at the border when I drove across. My other option was to take the cash. That option was worth far less than the value of the car but with no hassle and no out-of-pocket costs. I accepted the cash option. Guess how much money I won after the exchange rate was factored in? You got it. $17,277.28 to the penny. My mind was blown. I could not believe how this had worked. My focus and energy had paid off big time!

You would think two things would happen here now that I had seen this miraculous turn of events. I would pay off my debt and spend every morning for the rest of my life doing the manifesting ritual I had learned.

I did not.

I did not pay off my debt.

I gave the money to someone in my life who convinced me they deserved it more—and I kept the debt. On top of that (and this really baffled me), I never tried to manifest anything in this manner again with this method until many years later. It's as if someone gave me a magic lamp, I asked for my wish (of which I had unlimited wishes), got it, then threw the lamp away and ran.

Why did I do this? Why did I self-sabotage?

Looking back, it is obvious. I did not believe I was worthy. I did not believe I deserved a good, happy, or blessed life. I was so full of unprocessed shame, ugly thoughts, and sadness that there was no space for a new car or any kind of winnings. My sabotage setpoint kicked in and that was that.

Visualization Hack: *My Perfect Day*

This exercise will help you get clear on what would be dreamy.

Pretend it's two to five years in the future. Start with waking up and feeling what it's like to eagerly begin a new day. What does it feel like when your foot hits the floor? Do you go for a coffee and stare out the window? What's the view? Are you physically fit? When you think about work, do you get excited? Are you content? Overjoyed? Think about your bank account and how good it feels to have more than enough in the account. Visualize cashing a check or the numbers on your bank app.

Picture the entire day in beautiful detail. What do you do? Where are you? How do you feel? (You can write this out first if that's easier.)

Visualization Hack: *50 million*

Imagine that you won 50 million dollars today when you checked your lottery ticket.

What comes up for you? (You can also write this exercise out but remember to also visualize.)

Do you feel guilty? (We'll need to change that!) Do you pay your bills? Buy a boat? What would happen if you won? Seriously. Do this exercise and notice how you feel. This will highlight areas you can work on healing and any set points you may have in place around money and finances.

Visualization Hack: *Old Friend*

Picture running into an old friend in the airport five years from now and all your dreams, visualizations, and affirmations have come true. Now picture what you would say to them. Tell them about your home, your health, income, whatever you want. This exercise is powerful for visualizing because you are imagining all of the good stuff has already happened, so it puts you in a current vibration of success and happiness.

Help, My Visualizations Aren't Working!

But what if this isn't working either? What if things are happening slowly or not at all? Have you ever tried to visualize and just can't?

What if you are paralyzed and can't get into action? What if you have been doing the affirmations, the gratitude, and the visualizing and you are still stuck? What if nothing seems to work?

"It's never too late to recognize what has been holding you back and remove it."

- JESSICA HIGDON

In my experience, as you release the unprocessed emotions and sabotage beliefs (the "hidden stuff") which are anchored deep and vibrating at a very low frequency, it will become easier. Imagine again running chest-deep in water with weights on your ankles. *Until* you identify and release the stuff that's slowing you down, it's going to be like trying to get out of quicksand.

No matter how many times you speak, "I am worthy of success," into the mirror, there is still that nagging feeling that you are not worthy. No matter how many times you visualize abundance, there is still not enough money to pay all the bills, let alone have all the "things and experiences" you want to have. Or maybe it is an underlying feeling of guilt, feeling like you are in trouble all the time or people are mad at you. Maybe there is a deep-seated fear to shine, or you wake up anxious. Perhaps there is some deep-down anger that you know is there but don't want to face or don't know how to release. Fear of success, fear of failure, an overwhelming feeling of "why bother" or life isn't fair. Maybe you get this sick feeling every time you are praised or have the opportunity to shine, maybe you just can't get past a certain level, rank, or income. No matter how many books you read on changing your habits, positive mindset, and being fearless, you just keep coming back to the same place *or* the flight path is changing but at an excruciatingly slow pace.

Stay encouraged! As you release your unprocessed emotions this will shift.

Recently, my client Lisa and I released all her unprocessed emotions and many of her sabotage beliefs. She reported back to me that she was manifesting at a powerful pace. It felt as though everything she was speaking out was coming to fruition. She said she was at the tennis courts the other day and realized they had forgotten to bring tennis balls. She said, "What we really need are tennis balls" and no less than a minute later, a guy drove up in his car. He had a bag full of tennis balls and said, "You look like you could use some balls." Just like that.

Then she shared about her recent vacation when she continually told her family to slow down, stop rushing or someone would slip and get a concussion. Within a couple of days, she did that very thing. Slipped and got a concussion.

This works no matter what you are speaking out. What are you currently speaking out? What do you want more of? Continue to release and affirm, express gratitude and visualize, and have patience in the process. If things haven't visibly started to shift, they will soon.

After the Release and Reset

After you have released all of your unprocessed emotions, unpacked your sabotage beliefs, reset your setpoints, *plus* added positive daily habits which raise your vibration, you will notice a few changes. These changes will be subtle for some, and transformatively different for others.

You may no longer respond to others as you have in the past. You might feel more neutral and without a strong emotional reaction. Understand that you used to have buttons that people and incidents would push. Now you don't. Now you get to show up quite simply, as *you*. As God designed you. You will notice more allowing and more intention.

The Power of Choice

Although you won't respond in your old ways emotionally, some old habitual thoughts may pop up. This is your opportunity to be curious and choose a new way of responding.

One of my clients and I had released a bundle of sabotage beliefs and trapped emotions.

A short time later, she was having lunch with a friend who commented on what she chose from the menu. Basically, inferring my client had made a bad choice. Normally, this would have caused her to shut down, feel sick, and push down anger. She would have interpreted it to mean she was fat, incompetent, and stupid.

However, when her friend commented, instead of feeling all the usual feelings, she simply noticed that she didn't like it. Instead of shutting down, she said, "When you comment about my food choices, I find it hurtful and offensive. It feels as if you are commenting on my weight or my health, and I don't like it."

"Although you don't respond in your old ways emotionally, some old habitual thoughts may pop up."

The friend was shocked. She said she had never thought of it that way and was trying to be helpful but could see how it was hurtful. She promised to do better in the future.

This was a major victory! What is important to note here is that she chose to address her friend and the situation in a new way. She admitted she was tempted to respond her old way but chose new ground. The lack of a trigger helped but the old way of responding (a habit) was still tempting.

Part of this process is also relearning how to show up. You will notice you are not responding in your normal way. You will still have to choose to do something different. Believe it or not, some people become entrenched in the habit of feeling sad, mad, hurt, or lonely. When the old familiar feeling disappears, it's important to have intention around how you want to feel and what is true.

I'll share just a couple more personal stories to highlight what I mean here.

Mother's Day has traditionally been a tough day for me. I am a stepmom. I am blessed with the most amazing stepchildren. I consider them my gift from God. I consider them my children. I have always also been aware that I am their "bonus" mom, not their "real" mom. (They have an amazing mom.) I am close with the kids, and they are also extremely close to their mom. I was never conflicted over this. I love that I have been able to play the role in their lives that I have been blessed with. My husband and I were lucky enough to have both children live with us full-time for most of their high school years. I love being a bonus mom and have always tried to do the best I could while respecting their mom, too.

My husband and I were never able to have children of our own. We had a couple of miscarriages and then somewhere along the way stopped trying and fully embraced our perfect family of four. Exactly as God had intended. Still, even with all my counseling experience, coaching wisdom, and knowledge about emotion, I always felt a bit sad and out of place on Mother's Day. Often, I would go into another room and cry, feeling deep down like some kind of failure or loss. I tried to have no expectations of the children—I would cry disproportionately if they brought me flowers or a card. Somehow, I felt unworthy.

This year, after all the unprocessed emotions had been released and my sabotage beliefs were few and far between, I found myself standing at the kitchen sink on Mother's Day. It was noon, and neither of the kids had called or texted. My first response was the thought that they were likely still sleeping, it was Sunday after all, and they are in their early 20s living their own lives. I was not upset (in previous years I might have been) but peaceful, thinking to myself how much I loved them both.

Then it happened, that old ugly thought: *They don't love me.*

Out of nowhere.

These are the moments I am talking about. These moments are where the automatic thoughts pop in and we choose.

So, I simply asked, *Is that true?* In total transparency, I felt myself yearning a little bit for the old Jennie who would have felt sad and sorry for herself but pretend everything was okay.

When I asked myself if it was true, I got a clear NO. They love me. I thought of them hugging me. I thought of all the sweet conversations and moments. I thought of all the *"I love yous"* and *"thank yous"* and I knew. This self-loathing habit was over.

But I had to choose and *that* surprised me. I hoped with all the work I had done; I would never have another self-sabotage thought again. But, from time to time, they will pop up. At these times you must be vigilant.

Even after everything had been released, there was still a decision to choose the old path or forge a new one. This decision for some is a new skill. It is important to be aware of it moving forward, so you can choose to fight the good fight.

The Power Questions

As you heal and release, get curious. Ask yourself these five power questions.

1. **What do I want?**
2. **Is that (your assumption about the situation) true?**
3. **What is important in the long run here?**
4. **How can I do better in this scenario?**

5. What would be a new way to respond to this?

Welcome, unpack, and release those old thoughts like steam from a pot.

When something happens that triggers emotions or old beliefs, use the ALARM method or use your unpacking motion to clear that stuck energy. Remember, it's a gift when we discover something new to release. Whatever you do, don't push it down, ignore it or resist it. Help those emotions flow through as they are meant to. Do what you need to but stop feeding the monster!

If you have ever read, "The Easy Way to Quit Smoking" by Alan Carr you would understand this reference.

There was a time when I was a smoker. Someone recommended this book to me. I could not fathom what could be said in this book that would work when everything else I had ever tried had not helped me quit but I was willing to give it a shot.

I had smoked since I was 14 years old. I had said every day since I started, "This is my last pack." It has been over a decade since I quit, but at the time it was all I could think about, and I hated myself for it. I didn't know about unprocessed emotions. I didn't know I was sabotaging myself. I didn't know I could reset my autopilot or that a RAS filter even existed. Every time I tried to quit, that darn alarm would go off and I would fail.

"Pull up, pull up. Terrain ahead, terrain ahead."

You see, the author likened nicotine to food for a monster. You could kill the monster by not feeding it any nicotine. But if you gave it any nicotine whatsoever, the monster would grow large again and you would have to start all over. It was a great visual. Each time I thought of having a cigarette, I would think of that darn monster getting big again. Instead, I imagined the monster growing weaker and smaller each day. I did not want to make it big again.

Along with that concept, the author cleverly pairs the idea of freedom. When we quit something, we often think of what we are losing. For me, smoking was my friend, my crutch. It was there for me when I was sad, needed a break, wanted to celebrate, party, or feel sorry for myself. It was my friend. I could not imagine losing it. Carr describes gaining freedom instead of losing something. Quietly, throughout the whole book, he plants the message. Gain your freedom. Not a loss but a gain.

By the end of the book and some miraculous prayer, my smoking days were over. I realize now, the author cleverly reset my RAS filter to see where there was freedom versus loss. That book gave my autopilot a new destination and in doing so, shut off the alarm.

The point is, I still had to choose. I had to choose not to feed the monster. You will have to choose, too.

Choose not to hold onto anger, choose a more positive thought, choose to unpack. Choose to show up differently. Choose freedom. It's not easy but it's possible. It is my wish for you, that as you move toward a higher frequency life, where your tractor beam is pulling in greater abundance, peace, joy, and laughter, you will notice new sabotage limits to reset and hidden emotions that are finally ready to heal. And you will notice new opportunities to choose more, grow more, and become aware more.

Put another way, you will notice the opportunity to unpack, release, reset, and SELF SABOTAGE NO MORE.

ABOUT THE AUTHOR

Jennie Potter grew up in a small beach town in Western Canada. After years of spiraling into self-loathing and self-sabotage, Jennie knew she had to change her direction. She finally sought help and found the answers to healing through faith, counseling school, coaching certificates, and personal growth.

In addition to a background as an entrepreneur, Jennie has a bachelor's degree in psychology, earned a diploma at counseling college, and is a certified John Maxwell coach. She has invested thousands of hours in reading, coursework, study, and practice in the areas in which she teaches and helps clients today.

Jennie is obsessed with helping people identify and remove the hidden emotional blocks that hold people back from living their best lives. She is passionate about identifying tangible ways to release and move through limiting beliefs, emotions, fear, and negative mindsets. She thrives on helping others achieve through faith, vision, release, manifestation, exploration, and powerful daily habits— empowering others in applying actionable ways to break through, use their God-given gifts and shine fully as the light they were made to be in this world.

Today, Jennie is a Future-Self Coach for entrepreneurs, a faith-filled trainer in the network marketing space, a published author, and an inspirational speaker. She lives on the west coast of Vancouver Island, in British Columbia with her husband Dave, their kids, and two furbabies.

Let's Connect!

Facebook: MrsJenniePotter

Instagram: @Jennie_Potter

Website: JenniePotter.com

By visiting my website, you'll discover my latest tools for helping you self-sabotage no more, how to become a coaching client should you desire a deeper level of assistance, and more.

Finally... Thank you so much for reading.

Is now an okay time to ask for a favor?

I would LOVE and greatly appreciate it if you would consider leaving an honest review of my book on your favorite book-buying platform.

Now available at: JenniePotter.com

Made in United States
Orlando, FL
23 June 2023

34453412R00065